Parenting
Teenagers

Parenting Teenagers

20 Tough Questions and Answers

Lois Leiderman Davitz, Ph.D.
Joel R. Davitz, Ph.D.

Paulist Press
New York / Mahwah, N.J.

Cover design by Diego Linares
Book design by Lynn Else

LIBRARY OF CONGRESS CATALOGING-IN-PUBLICATION DATA

Davitz, Lois Jean.
    Parenting teenagers : 20 tough questions and answers / Lois Leiderman Davitz, Joel R. Davitz.
        p. cm.
    ISBN 0-8091-4100-0 (alk. paper)
    1. Parent and teenager. 2. Parenting. I. Davitz, Joel Robert. II. Title.
    HQ799.15 .D39 2003
    649'.125—dc21

                                                            2003001683

Published by Paulist Press
997 Macarthur Boulevard
Mahwah, New Jersey 07430

www.paulistpress.com

Printed and bound in the United States of America

Contents

Introduction

To Parents

Parenting teenagers is a lot tougher than it was a couple of generations ago. When teenagers today say that life is a lot different for them than it was for their parents, we think they're probably right! Monumental changes in lifestyles and social behaviors have occurred in a relatively short time.

What does this mean for parents of teenagers today? They not only have to deal with the normal problems and crises of adolescent development, but they also face a complex set of expectations that make parenting even more difficult. For example, they are expected to be loving and accepting but not overly possessive; involved but not overinvolved; firm but not authoritarian; supportive but not overprotective.

This book is an effort to sort out some of the daunting questions parents face. To accomplish this goal we surveyed several hundred parents of teenagers to identify their major concerns. On this basis we identified the twenty most frequently asked questions and these provide the core issues we will discuss.

The tough answer to each question is meant to serve as a guideline for your behavior. Every family is unique. We know that each of you should be and is the best judge of what is right and appropriate for your family. Therefore, we're not going to present pat answers or formulas. Rather, we're going to talk about certain factors and issues every parent might well consider, drawing on our professional experience as psychologists and educators and on our own mistakes in child-rearing!

Parenting at any age is a challenge. It's a little more stimulating, exciting, and adventuresome with a teenager.

Lois Leiderman Davitz, Ph.D.
Joel R. Davitz, Ph.D.

The tough question:

1 | *"Am I a good parent?"*

"It bothers me a lot whether I am a good parent," a mother of a fifteen-year-old boy and a seventeen-year-old girl told us. "I think what I do is right. I suppose one never knows. It all seems unpredictable. Things change from day to day. I'll say something and they'll flare up. The next time it's all sweetness and light.

"I didn't have terrific parents. Maybe that's why I'm so concerned about my parenting. My husband's mom and dad were just OK. There were a lot of kids in the family; his older brothers and sisters sort of took over the parenting job. He was the youngest.

"We really care about being good role models. I sometimes feel guilty about things that happen. I don't want my kids resenting their father or me when they grow up. I don't want to keep thinking I should have behaved differently.

"I'm always reading articles about what one should and shouldn't do with kids. Every one of the so-called experts has an ax to grind. It makes me wonder if I should take child-rearing so seriously. Does everyone go through periods when they worry they're not the greatest role models? Does everyone feel some guilt about what they do? Will my kids someday tell me what they thought about me as a mother?"

Mrs. M., mother of two teenagers

The tough answer:

Worry about how well you're doing as a parent? Feel guilty when things just don't work out or there is a crisis? Wonder how your behavior will affect your teenager later in life? How well we understand and empathize with these feelings! Over the years we've often been asked if we ever had doubts about what we did as parents. Did we think we had the right answers for what and what not to do? After all this was our field of expertise. For over thirty-five years we worked with hundreds and hundreds of youngsters. Was it possible we, too, made mistakes?

With our own children, initially, we thought we knew what we were doing, the right way to behave, the appropriate kinds of reactions to make, but the reality is that there were *many* times when we were as bewildered as any parent. And we assure you, Mrs. M., every parent we know has at one time or another shared your self-doubts, concerns, and guilt. Certainly, we have.

Every child is uncharted territory. The needs of one youngster aren't going to be the needs of another. Parenting teenagers, we have finally come to realize, is going to involve a mixture of intuition, confusion, doubt, guilt, knowledge, and uncertainty as well as a great deal of joy and pleasure.

The one certainty about raising kids is summed up in the statement of one of our sons when he was well into adulthood. We talked to him about our child-rearing during his teenage years. Were we hard to live with? What kinds of mistakes did we make? Were there things we could have done that would have made his life happier or easier? Aware of our concern and obvious tension, he became very reassuring.

"You did just fine. Stop worrying. You could have been worse," he assured us. And then he paused, before adding with obvious amusement, *"Just remember, to err is parental."*

No matter who you are, no matter the depths of your knowledge and the strength of your convictions, mistakes are inevitable. There will be moments when you will totally shock yourself, saying things and behaving in a way you never dreamed possible. When emotions are high and there is tension, all the good values and ideals you may have disappear.

If this weren't the case, how could I, a mature, generally controlled adult, supposedly with education and knowledge, lose my cool one evening many, many years ago. I ran around the kitchen with a broom chasing a teenage son who had been bugging me nonstop. After I calmed down, and became more rational, I thought this couldn't have been me. Decades later, I still find what I did hard to accept.

Hopefully, I assumed this event would be a repressed memory for him. It certainly wasn't as I discovered recently when this same son, now a father, thirty years later, reminded me that it was neither ladylike nor mature of me to have to run around the kitchen with a broom in hand. "Of course," he added, "you didn't catch me."

And there was the time when another son showed his composition to his father. He had worked long and hard on the paper and expected glowing praise for his effort.

"Just make any corrections, Dad," he said.

His request was taken literally, a major mistake, as his father reviewed each sentence, every word, until the four pages were completely obscured from top to bottom with red-penciled corrections.

"Wasn't it any good?"

"No, it needs to be completely redone."

"Nothing I ever do is right," he said in a tone of shock mixed with despair.

"That's not what I said. You asked me for my help."

"Yes, but I didn't expect this," he answered, angrily crushing the sheets in his closed fist.

The relationship between an adolescent and a parent is fragile. Some truths need to be glossed over. The balance can be swayed so easily. Tempers on either side can get out of control over trivialities. One father recalls the one and only time he ever struck his teenage daughter. "We were having an argument. She kept making taunting remarks, stood in the doorway of the kitchen saying things that shouldn't have been said. She refused to stop. I struck her. I was immediately horrified at what I did. I was so damn ashamed of having lost control."

Lapses of parental maturity are inevitable; otherwise, there never would have been an emotional evening of bitter words erupting over the significance and influence of Elvis Presley mania. Elvis died. Newspapers and reporters carried on about the singer's relevance to teenage life and his impact on every American.

"Elvis Presley has changed **all our lives,**" one son announced solemnly at dinner. "He's been a *major* influence in the behavior of every person," he continued, paraphrasing the commentators.

The rest of his speech was cut off.

"Utter nonsense," Joel replied angrily. "I never heard the man sing. He has not affected my life. And I couldn't care less what he did. In fact, if you want to know my opinion about Elvis and others like him, I'll tell you."

"You're not being honest."

"Honest? Who the hell is he anyway?"

A lot more was said as tempers got totally out of hand and accusations were shouted. Obviously the Elvis argument involved a lot more than his influence and undoubtedly triggered off something to do with father-son authority and a teenage son's challenge of power. In looking back, we can only be grateful that the Elvis battle stopped short of physical combat.

In many ways it became clear to us that Elvis Presley *did* change our lives. We learned the importance of remembering to remain a little more mature in some situations. We didn't forget, nor did our son. A treasured Christmas present from him when he was well into adulthood was a life-sized plaster head of Elvis Presley.

Thus, it is our very strong belief that concerned parents should simply face the fact that errors are bound to occur. There will be moments when your behavior will be a lot less mature and less rational than the teenager's. At these times you certainly won't win prizes for being a great role model.

The second conclusion we have come to is that, at times, no matter what you do, you are going to be accused of being wrong. We believe this testing of a parent is a stage teenagers must go through—a rite of passage on their way to becoming adults. When teenagers start blaming you for what you're doing or what you've done, it's a good idea to pause and reflect on how you blamed *your* parents, perhaps for the very same thing you're being blamed for doing or saying now.

The third conclusion we eventually came to was *stop comparing*.

We tried our best to stop imagining how wonderful other teenagers were in their homes, how perfect other parents were in comparison to our inadequacies. When all these comparisons were safely out of the way, we were able to take a giant leap toward establishing a real relationship with our teenagers that didn't focus on guilt, role models, or concerns about whether we were being good or bad parents. None of that mattered.

What really mattered was our trying to be as honest as we could with ourselves. Concretely, this meant making our best effort to admit we were wrong when it was clear to us that we had made a mistake. This wasn't always easy for us, but in our own stumbling way, we learned to admit being wrong without being defensive. After plenty of trial and error, we finally learned the magic power of the simple statement, "I'm sorry; I was wrong."

After our sons were fathers we talked about ourselves as parents and what they thought was the *most* important thing we did. Quite independently and without hesitation, each son told us that the greatest thing we did was to make sure *the door was always open*. We were always willing to talk and to be available to listen. No matter what happened—a rock that was tossed through a glass storm door in a gesture of defiance, a disappearance from home for an entire evening after a threat to leave and never return—both sons knew deep down that grudges were not held. The door would always remain open.

Their metaphor of ***keeping the door open*** underscores our philosophy of communication and understanding that we believe all parents must engrave indelibly on their minds. Accept that you are going to feel guilty sometimes for your irrational behavior. Accept that your teenagers are going to behave in ways that you may find totally unacceptable. Face the fact that some of your behavior on certain occasions will leave much to be desired. In the long run, what will really count is not a specific bit of behavior, a particular action, or words said that should have been left unsaid, but your overall sense of caring and communication—keeping the door open no matter what.

The tough question:

2 | *"For the parent of a teenager, what's most important to remember?"*

Our sons' adolescence finally came to an end. The bumpy stages, awkward moments, hilarious laughter, sadness and blues, ups and downs, fun times and crises were no longer a part of daily life. It came as a bit of a shock when we saw empty beds and realized that our teenagers were out of the house. Wasn't it only yesterday that we brought them home as newborns from the hospital? Time passing much too quickly is a disturbing sensation that every parent experiences.

The toughest stage of raising children is adolescence. Little ones are happy and content with a lot of loving and tender care. From about seven until twelve, everything is discovery and excitement. When children are adults, of course you're involved and caring, but decisions about their lives are out of your control. And with grandchildren, no matter the age, everything they do is absolutely wonderful and perfect, whether it is active rebellion, playing four notes in vague order on a trumpet, or swimming one length of a swimming pool without gasping for air.

Thus, one of the biggest challenges in your life is going to be during those teenage years when you will have to marshal all your wits and wisdom to stay sane. It is possible. Providing something more than tender loving care is going to be the key to your success. That extra dimension is what we call *rational parenting*. It is not a matter of special technical knowledge, but rather a process involving certain human qualities.

The tough answer:

The process must be incorporated into everyday life. Don't wait until a problem occurs to become a rational parent, only to take off that guise when life is once again smooth. Rather, give-and-take, sharing realities, active encouragement and respect for individuality, indeed the entire process of rational parenting must become an intrinsic part of your day-to-day interactions.

Know yourself as a parent and be true to yourself. Forget about the ideal model of a perfect parent. Don't worry about all the mistakes you made or will make. It's far more important to be genuinely yourself, with your own faults and shortcomings, but also with the honesty that can only be achieved by being true to yourself.

Remember to get in touch with how your adolescent experiences his or her world. In seeking to understand your teenager, be a parent who empathizes, but doesn't analyze. Make a commitment to listen without interrupting, without pre-judging, without trying to manipulate or outwit your adolescent. And by all means share your opinions and your feelings about whatever the topic is being discussed. A good way to practice real shared dialogue is when you are discussing topics about which neither of you feels very emotionally involved.

Stop the blame game with your teenager. Remember that in parenting no one profits from proving someone else is guilty.

Express your feelings openly and honestly, but own your own feelings. Don't project the blame for your own feelings onto your adolescent.

Confront the problems, conflicts, and disagreements you run into with your adolescent. Don't ignore problems, hoping they will take care of themselves. They won't. This doesn't mean you have to overreact every time there is something amiss in your youngster's life. However, staying alert and concerned is just part of the role of a caring parent. When something comes up that really concerns your adolescent, keep your eye on the problem at hand.

Particularize; don't generalize in dealing with any problems your teenager faces. In working on solutions, don't give big lectures or pep talks. Rather, make your suggestions specific, practical, and down to earth.

Be willing to take a reasonable chance on your adolescent's growing maturity. Value the differences between you and your teenager, and do whatever you can to encourage and reinforce his or her independence and individuality. At the same time, remember to respect your own individuality and independence.

Make your expectations clear and explicit with regard to the small things of family living. Whenever you have the chance, regardless of how minor the opportunity seems to be, encourage and reinforce your adolescent's striving for independence and individuality.

The tough question:

3 | *"What are the most valuable gifts I can give to my teenager?"*

Our weekly sessions with a group of parents were ending. A much-needed break was in order. Besides, the holiday season was uppermost in everyone's mind. "Why is December so frantic?" asked one woman. "You would think I had enough time to shop in the last eleven months."

"Harder and harder each year," complained another parent. "What do you get an adolescent who has everything? A gift certificate shows about as much thoughtfulness to your own kid as a new box of breakfast cereal."

Kids have everything, the parents lamented. That's the problem with this era. "My kids can't even drum up a wish," noted one parent. Everyone shook their heads at the sorry state of affairs.

Christmas gifts have gotten bigger, more electronic, and considerably more expensive than when our adult sons were teenagers. Parents today struggle with decisions. We certainly aren't going to extol the simple life. We do not want to delude you or ourselves that presents on holidays don't matter. Of course they do, and we simply have to accept the fact that material gifts are a part of our lives.

But in the long run, there are other, nonmaterial gifts that we can give our teenagers that are infinitely more meaningful than any video game or fancy sweater.

The tough answer:

We shall make no apologies for providing a sentimental but tough answer to this question. In all honesty, this kind of reply could not have been written when we were younger and the parents of teenagers. It does take age, maturity, and *a lot of living experience* to realize that the best gifts we can give to teenagers are three in number.

We believe that the number one gift you can give to your teenager is the sense that *he or she is special.* Whether you have one child or several, each is special in his or her own way. Every youngster deserves somewhere in the world where he or she occupies a unique place, and this place is in your home and heart.

We're quite aware in writing this that some people will be uncomfortable with sentimentality. In a day and age where science and technology reign as king, sentimentality can make some of us cringe. We probably would have agreed with you decades ago. We've come a long way because we truly believe that being special is the most important gift one can give to a teenager.

"Of course my daughter knows how I feel. She is special," one mother told us.

Our response was, "Are you so sure? Have you told her? It's not just feeling this way that matters. Have you let your teenager know your feelings?"

The second most important gift for your teenager is making sure they know that their home, *no matter how big or small, is a special refuge*, a place to come to when they are bouncing with joy or when everything in the outside world isn't so perfect. Every one of us needs our "cave," a warm, secure place where we can be ourselves without any conditions, judgments, and evaluations—just our being is enough.

The third gift we can give our youngster is *total, unqualified forgiveness*. This does not mean that we will approve everything they do, nor that we can't make suggestions. This does not mean they won't do things we will believe are totally wrong. But it does mean that we make sure no matter what, we are ready to forgive and, more importantly, to help them move on with their lives. With forgiveness for transgressions must come a healthy dose of forgetting so we can honestly accept when a new leaf is turned.

The tough question:

4 | *"How do I establish a close relationship with my teenager?"*

"We get the feeling that our job now in life is to support them, have food on the table, provide clothes, and save for college. Sometimes we feel 'used.' There are days when 'hello' and 'goodbye' is the sum total of our conversation. The biggest discussion we've had in a week was about when he wanted the car and when my daughter wanted the car. After they turn thirteen, do kids forget parents exist? Our kids are fifteen and seventeen. We figure the way we're going now we'll be lucky if they remember our names. Oh, we do sound sour, don't we? We used to have a close relationship and do things together. No more."

Parent of two teenagers

The tough answer:

Yes, you do sound sour, hurt, disappointed, and a little or maybe a lot angry. However, you really are rather mild compared to some of the opinions we've heard about life with a teenager. Parents have called themselves doormats, nothing more than wallets; kids have been described as a financial worry, a responsibility without rewards. But we want you to know, when asked if they loved their kids, every single one of these complaining parents was astonished we would even bring up such a notion.

"Of course, I adore my kids," said one mother just after she told us she was getting migraines with the constant noise and the annoyed expression her son gave her when she asked him if he minded taking his friends somewhere else to play drums.

"That's a strange question to ask," a father told us. "My kids are very important to me. The financial responsibility is something I worry about. The second mortgage I will have to take out when my daughter starts college. The strain I will feel trying to scrape enough to put aside tuition and room and board for the second one a couple of years later. Nowadays, kids are an enormous financial responsibility."

Relationships with adolescents, for the most part, involve chores, responsibilities, problems, conflicts, and the business of living without an equal amount of employment. We wondered about this heavy-handed pattern that parents slip into without awareness. Going over our family photo albums provided us with some clues. Snapshots taken of our kids and us when they were small show laughing children and parents, family picnics, camel rides at the zoo. My, weren't we a happy, contented foursome?

Later albums that covered the time when our children were teenagers are quite different. There are fewer and fewer simply happy pictures of parents and children just having fun together. This change in our photo albums reflected the changes in relating to our children, as they grew older. It was no longer just a matter of having fun together. The more serious aspects of living became increasingly more important.

Clearly, parenting had taken on a solemn note of responsibilities. When our kids wanted to enjoy themselves, they sought out their own friends as companions. When relationships between parents and adolescents focus primarily on the business of living to the exclusion of anything that might be done together just for enjoyment, the relationship automatically slips into a sober stance. Everything is problem-oriented and the goal is to solve the problem. An ideal spring afternoon for a six-year-old might be playing catch with dad. For a six-teen-year-old, it's not as much.

It's natural for duties and responsibilities to take over. The teenager is busy; the parents are occupied with their own activities. The most togetherness many parents can manage with their kids is watching a video and even that is less likely. The teenagers want to sit with their own pals in the family room and are not going to be ecstatic when parents drift into the room to share in the fun and games. The age gap widens far more than just chronological years.

We remember being aware of the shift in family togetherness. Our kids adored playing Monopoly when they were children. As teenagers, they would undoubtedly have been aghast if we had suggested, "Let's have a fun-filled Saturday night Monopoly game."

We worried that we ran the risk of losing them to schedules, duties, chores, responsibilities, in short, the dynamics of their own lives. What happens with teenagers and their parents is what so often happens in marriages. People marry for fun and enjoyment and the chance to be together. Over time the business of life takes over and all the fun and games are distant memories. The same holds true for children.

As youngsters, the relationship consists of a lot of fun and games besides the chores. This subtly changes with adolescence. Youngsters want to play games and have fun with friends their own age. Of course, we could no longer sit with them building sand-castles on a beach as we did when they were small.

And yet we weren't willing to give up completely. There were things we could do that would become peak memories for us and, hopefully, for our teenagers. We began planning. We knew that we had to think of some activities away from the home; otherwise, old stereotype behaviors would take over.

The key words were share and enjoy. We were determined to make shared activities with our adolescent a regular part of our lives together. This eliminated such things as sitting watching television together, meeting at the dinner table to go over problems, and having discussions about their lives, music lessons, smoking, sex, or any of a variety of other topics that might lead to conflict. We wanted time together that didn't revolve around problems, our advice, and long talks that ended up with us in the mentor or authority role. To accomplish this goal, we knew that we had to escape into a new situation to break the set roles each of us had fallen into. We knew that our kids probably preferred to spend time with their friends, so naturally when we proposed something they either refused or complied begrudgingly, thus sapping all the enjoyment out of whatever we did together. Still, we were determined not to give up, not to accept the excuse that kids need to be with other kids.

Our initial suggestion was not greeted enthusiastically, though there was some relenting when we told them why we wanted to plan something special to recapture the fun we had when they were small. We let them come up with the idea, which was for a bicycle trip over the summer. One son was sixteen, the other twelve. We left for a month-long cycling trip.

Within a few days we acquired a totally new perspective about one son. Where had he learned to repair bicycles? Where had he learned his skill finding routes? Where had he learned how to help us maneuver our way through traffic over dirt roads, how to change and patch tires? The entire emotional tone of our relationship changed. We were suddenly dependent on him for a lot of decisions.

We do not feel this could have been accomplished in the home setting. Of course, the activity you decide to do with your adolescent may not involve anything as major as undertaking a bicycle trip. The important thing is not what you do or where you do it, but the process of sharing in something together that is totally for fun. It doesn't have to be for weeks or even a whole day.

It may be only for a few hours, but make the most of the time. Share an enjoyable experience so that you have a chance to discover depths in each other you may never have realized were there. Just remember to go slowly. You may meet resistance. You many even meet a shrug of the shoulders and a scoffing, "What are we going to do?" Don't let this deter you. Remember, when you break old habits of behaving, it's not always easy. It will be bumpy. However, once you have gone off together and not worried about allowances, duties, car keys, lawns, cleaning up a room, homework, or assignments of any sort, but have given yourselves a chance to laugh and to share something, you will discover a new pleasure in your relationship with each other. Memories of such experiences will last the rest of your lives.

The tough question:

5

"How do I know when it is the right time to step in and take a more active role in my teenager's life?"

"My daughter is thirteen. My son is sixteen," Mr. O. told us. "I know all the reasons why parents should give their teenagers freedom, let them become independent, cut loose from the family so they can grow up. It bothered me when I was a teenager, having my parents breathe down my neck. I have more problems letting go with my daughter than with my son. I feel protective about her. I feel protective about him, too. But he seems stronger, more sure of himself.

"Knowing when to step in and when to cut loose is tough. My wife goes to one extreme; I suppose I go to the other. We've got to find a middle ground. That makes sense for everyone. But the rules one goes by of when to step in and to stay out of their affairs aren't spelled out anywhere. I can't let my kids make some kinds of decisions. I think I've heard it a thousand times

from my son, 'Get off my back.' My daughter pouts. 'Dad, I'm
not a little girl any longer. You've got to let me go.'

"I'll concede a point. They shouldn't have my wife and me
hanging over their shoulders, keeping them under lock and key.
They're not to be kept in a glass cage with us monitoring their
every move. On the other hand, I can't turn a deaf ear and a
blind eye. They have limited experiences with the world. That
makes sense. They're far too trusting. I just find it difficult to sit
back and do nothing when I see things I don't like, threats of
danger or whatever."

Mr. O., father of two teenagers

The tough answer:

"How was the party last night?" we asked our son, who was
seventeen-years-old at the time.

"Fine."

"Who was there?"

"People."

"Don't get fresh."

"Who's getting fresh? You asked me a question. OK, 'kids.'"

"What kids?"

"You don't know some. Some you know."

"Your age? Older, younger?"

"I didn't ask."

"We just wanted to know."

"Are you taking a census?"

"OK, how about food. Drinks?"

"Pizza. Coke."

"Was there beer?"

"You got to cut it. Next time I'll tape it all, take notes. I went
to a party. You know that. Why the third-degree examination?"

"Why are you so angry? All we are doing is asking a *few*

reasonable questions. What is so terribly wrong about parents wanting to know where their kid was and what he was doing?"

"You're darn right. There's a lot wrong. Can't you understand there are some parts of my life I want to keep for myself? Do you people have to know everything? Should I make an announcement next time I go to the bathroom?"

This dialogue, occurring decades ago, was unforgettable. An otherwise amiable, cooperative, delightful son turned into an ogre as we probed and queried about a party he had gone to and about which we had heard disturbing reports.

There was a time when our sons went to parties and returned home only too eager to volunteer or respond to our questions.

"What did you do?"

"We played 'pin the tail on the donkey.'"

"Did you pin a tail on?"

"I did. I even won jelly beans."

"How many?"

"Ten. Look." A hand was extended, the palm a myriad of colors from squashed jelly beans.

This kind of back-and-forth dialogue dramatically changes with adolescence when the teenager wants and deserves some privacy. On the other hand, the parent wants and deserves to be free from worry. In thinking back about our own experience, we realize that the barrage of questions we asked our teenage son didn't stem from a desire to know about the pizza or the kids but whether anything went on at the party that could be a cause for concern. Were there drugs? Were kids drinking? Did matters get out of hand? That was the information we wanted and our oblique questions were designed to get these facts. We didn't succeed.

How does a parent step in? *When* should a parent take a more active role in the teenager's life? Both of these questions are tied together. We have all the respect in the world for teenagers' judgments, intelligence, and sensitivity—and yet we know full well that, as grown up as they may seem, they are not adults. Mr. O. was quite right when he noted that his children don't have a lot of worldly experience. How could they at their age? And, because of this obvious fact, they are vulnerable.

Thus, we strongly believe there are times when a parent not only must step in but must do it with **both feet** and take charge. We recall one father who said that he suspected his son was using drugs. His wife agreed. She did what she thought was unthinkable. "I searched his room. I felt I had to know. We were right. Every time we asked him about drugs he denied everything. But we had evidence. We were right doing what we did. At the same time, deep down, I also know we were wrong. We violated his privacy. We searched his room. Would he ever trust us again? We had been spies, and, yet, if we didn't do anything, we ran the risk of him getting into big trouble."

Should they have stepped in? We felt they had no alternative. If they didn't, there might come a time when not only would they be forced to step in, but it may have been too late. Perhaps the way they went about the searches could have been different. But that was of less importance than their next step, which was to select a time and a place, free from interruptions, where everyone felt comfortable to talk about the problem. First and foremost, they had to let their son know it was a **shared** problem. No blame, no accusations, no histrionics but open and above-board honesty would be critical for their success in helping their son.

The turning point was their assurance to their son that this was a **shared** problem and he wasn't on trial. His parents weren't going to be prosecuting attorneys. They admitted their error in checking on his personal space, invading his privacy. This might have been wrong, but their concerns outweighed their good judgment.

When parents and the teenager **work together**, with the parent being totally honest, the teenager can let down his or her guard and become less defensive. In these kinds of situations, parents should show the same respect for the adolescent that they would to any adult in the family.

In our experience, we found that the best approach is to identify those things that we were worried about and to *limit* our intensive questioning to those situations. It's critically important to be selective in what you question your child about. Teenagers have a right to some privacy. We can't be all over them and their affairs. We remember one period when we were not only asking too many questions, but we were overly involved in everything.

Our son's room was a mess. He emerged from his room, neatly dressed, book bag in order, but inside the room the floor was littered. Friends told us of facing a similar problem. "I discovered leftover pizza—a week after the pizza was ordered—in the wastebasket," one mother reported. Another father stepped into his son's life to order him to grow hair. "A shaved head was intolerable," in his opinion.

The only time any parent wants to step in or take a more active role is in those situations where there is danger, the possibility of danger, or a problem of any magnitude. The reason that particular party upset us is because of what we had been told. Instead of evasive questioning, we should have come right to the point, which is what we started doing after the first instructive experience with that son.

When we decided to ease off on any of the topics or problems that weren't earthshaking or harmful, relationships dramatically improved. In the case of the messy room, the solution was so simple. The door was opened quickly once a week, clean clothes tossed on the bed, and the door quickly shut. The rule was that the door must be closed only because of the split-level floor plan where interiors of rooms were visible to others.

The message we sent was, "It's your room. If you want to live in a cyclone of possessions, that's your right." Eventually he tired of not being able to find what he wanted (favorite tapes, photos, books), and he cleaned everything up without our ever again having to comment. We became more than ever convinced of the policy of *not* making unnecessary issues about less than earthshaking matters. This eliminated unnecessary disagreements, long unhappy looks, and outbursts of temper on either side.

When we didn't like something that was happening, for example, when a friend of his was using drugs, we did our best to explain rationally our concerns to our son and to seek his help. Instead of going around the problem with all sorts of subterfuges or roundabout questions, we came right to the point and shared our worries.

Like many parents, we always had tried to put up a good front and to communicate confidence in our opinions. The shared approach does take a teenager aback and, in the beginning, may be less than comfortable for parents who are used to being authorities on everything in their child's life.

When children are young, parents are unquestioned authorities. "No, you will not finish all the Halloween candy. You will get a stomachache and have to go to the doctor. No, you will go to bed because if you don't get enough sleep you will get sick." We're always handing out bits of wisdom and pronouncements to young children.

Shifting roles and taking your teenager into your confidence as a friend working together for both your and their well-being means a drastic shift in parenting styles. Instead of being captain in your household, you're both colleagues, and colleagues do not have their rooms searched, their mail opened, telephone calls listened to—all things that parents have told us they have done in an effort to monitor what was going on in their teenager's life.

Although by and large we encourage parents to step in when there are genuine concerns and worries, we feel that this general statement has to be qualified. Save your energies for things that really matter. Learn to live with the reality that your teenager has a private life and a right to privacy. You don't have to know all the details about every social event, every dream, every thought, and every squeak of your child's life. Do what you can to hold back those emotionally loaded questions and challenges.

Holding back takes tremendous willpower and effort. If our sons didn't show up on time for dinner, we ate instead of tensely pacing rooms waiting for them. And upon their arrival we didn't demand all sorts of reasons for their being late. Save your efforts and your energies for those issues that really worry you.

Each family will have its own major concerns. Try to limit your invasion of your teenager's life to those things that you feel might be potentially threatening or hurtful. It's not that you want to make these topics the center of your relationship. That won't accomplish your goal. In fact, if your life begins centering on a few problem areas, your teenager is bound to tune out.

A straightforward "I'm worried" and an explanation why without accusations or blame can make an enormous difference in the emotional tone of the relationship. Just never forget that some psychological withdrawal is part of growing up. Be ready to listen and to offer support, but don't impose yourself unless there are real concerns that justify your stepping in and saying or doing something.

If you have been stepping in far too much and begin to retreat in an effort to have a reasonable and rational relationship, you may discover that the less you ask, the more information will be volunteered. As parents, we have to make sure we watch for cues from our children and share what they want to share. Learning to step in and when to interfere will sometimes make you feel like you're walking on a tightrope. You're eager to know, yet you're making yourself act with restraint. Just remember that an open, honest relationship will be your reward and well worth the effort on your part.

The tough question:

6 | *"How can I get my teenager to communicate with me?"*

"It is maddening. Every time I try to talk seriously with my kids, they give me this blank look. It doesn't take a genius to know what they're thinking. I only have to look at their feet, turned away, getting ready for that moment to escape.

"If it had always been like this, I could understand. It wasn't. My kids and I were always able to talk. Night after night I remember sitting on their beds, and we'd talk about what happened that day. They would tell me *everything*. I never had to push or even ask questions. When I would ask about something out of curiosity, I never felt like I was pounding a brick wall trying to get an answer.

"I'm no different from any other parent in this world. I want to do the best for my kids. How can I if we can't communicate? How else can a parent have any influence? I do not enjoy having them stare at me with a blank expression whenever I try to talk to them about anything more than trivia."

Mrs. F., mother of two teenagers

The tough answer:

We think, Mrs. F., that most parents share your same warm memories of those times when kids came home from a party and told us *everything* that happened, including how many potato chips they ate. Ten or eleven are ideal years. Youngsters report long tales of what happened to them in such great detail we have the feeling we were actually on the scene.

The "tuning off" and "tuning out" seems to come abruptly when kids enter their teens. However, we have to remember that turning away from parents as confidants doesn't necessarily have a negative connotation. Adolescence is a time of growing independence. The first step in that direction is **not** reporting every detail of their lives.

Now, with all the fancy psychological reasoning about maturation and developmental changes out of the way, let's be honest. It is *maddening* when a kid stands slouched against the kitchen sink, looking at us as if we were a piece of furniture. It's frustrating not to have meaningful verbal exchanges. Little scraps of information would mean so much to a parent.

Bits and pieces of information about what's going on in their lives would not only help us understand our adolescent but would also give us some clues about what kind of guidance is necessary. How can anyone parent a brick wall? How does one get a youngster to open up and really share?

When our children were teenagers we were pretty sure we knew all about the communication process, having researched and written on the subject. It came as a shock to us when we discovered that what we thought was communication one son called **the third degree**.

"You people are inquisitors," he told us.

We immediately defended our behavior. "We're just trying to get you to share what's happening in your life so we can be helpful parents."

"You call your questioning sharing? It's more like being on trial. I come home from a party and right away you're at me about who was there, what happened."

"What is so wrong? We want to find out about the evening."

"Why? You don't know most of the kids."

"You're our son. What goes on in your life is important to us. We certainly don't want you to disappear from our lives."

"Disappear because I don't tell you what went on at a party?"

We can't begin to tell you how many times versions of that dialogue were replayed in our home. In analyzing most teenager-parent communication, including ours, we have discovered the *first* stage is largely a one-way street, that is, the parent questions, and, hopefully, the teenager comes up with some sort of reply. If the reply indicates there isn't any danger, for example, drugs at the party, undesirable friends, to cite only two possible negatives, parents breathe a sigh of relief and the communication process swiftly comes to an end. However, if there is any suspicion of a problem, the *second* stage of communication consists of a lecture of some sort. If the dangers are perceived to be great enough, the parent quickly shifts into a role of prosecuting attorney, while the teenager becomes more and more defensive under the attack.

When we identified some of these patterns of communication, we were astonished. But what else were we doing when we bombarded our son with a series of questions about a party he recently attended?

"Who had drugs?"

"Who said there were drugs?"

"Did **you** try anything?"

"No."

"Let's hope you're telling me the God's honest truth. If you are not, well anyhow, I don't want you to be hanging out with those kids anymore." (The next stage of so-called communication is, more often than not, a list of right sorts of behaviors and lots of parental advice.)

What can parents do to engage teenagers in open communication without negative overtones? The first step might be for parents to ask themselves if they *really* want to listen or are they overeager to jump into the role of interrogator. We vividly remember making a communication discovery when our children were teenagers.

There was one period when, under the guise of casual interest, we bombarded them with questions. Of course, as psychologists we assumed we did this with discretion. It didn't take psychological training for us to finally realize their obvious determination to escape and to avoid at all costs all parental interest in their welfare.

We clearly were not making communication progress. Finally, more out of desperation than logic, we pulled back, going to the other extreme. We were the ones with stony silence, turning a deaf ear to anything that was said. One day we were stunned.

"I guess I don't mean much around here anymore. I might as well be a wall fixture," one son told us.

Astonished, we asked, "How did you come up with that nonsense?"

"You never ask me about what's going on in my life."

We stumbled onto some important insights.

1. *It's important to be interested but not to be an inquisitor.* It's important to listen sometimes without jumping in with all sorts of good, parental advice and suggestions that really are nothing more than old-fashioned lectures. Step back and listen. Sometimes, even though you might not like what you hear, hold off your judgments rather than jump in with critical evaluations at a sensitive moment.

2. *Teenager communication withdrawing makes developmental sense.* The same teenager, taciturn at times in our presence, would be voluble and talkative with friends. Adolescence is a time of shaping one's own self, getting a separate identity; thus, peer validation and peer interaction can be important and useful—maybe at times a bit more so than well-intentioned parental words.

3. *Above all, do what you can to tone down the lecturing even if you don't see it as lecturing.* Monologues are not going to be appreciated. In a previous section we talked about the new stage in relationships where the parent is a friend, not a prosecutor, not a judge, not a teacher. Good friends don't lecture or they don't last very long as good friends. Good friends do ***exchange*** information.

4. *Make sure that you really show you're listening.* Many times we were told and are still being told, "You don't understand and you don't listen." Parents are inevitably going to hear these comments. How do we show understanding when we have been given a privileged communication? How do we show we're really listening?

We think the answer is pretty straightforward. We show understanding by reserving judgment at that moment, thinking about what is being said and leaving *our* lives out of the discussion. We show we're really listening by not jumping in with lots of good advice until we're asked or if we ask is it "okay."

5. *Don't let your fears block communication.* The major stumbling block to parent-teenager communication is fear. If everything is going along fine with our kids, we don't sit and aggravate ourselves about communication. We may not even think about the issue. However, at the first hint of a problem, fear and concern leap into a parent's consciousness and the cycle of questioning and more questioning, attacks and defenses begins to take over.

Sometimes just being in the same room can be enough to block communication because of nonverbal reactions. Parents only have to sense a hint of danger and their voices change in speed, pitch, and loudness. Everything about the parents, from the way they stand or hold their hands, sends out messages of tension.

I, as the mother, was told many times it's ***never*** what I said but the sudden, high-pitched, somewhat squeaky tone that indicated my worrying. If you find yourself getting into that kind of worry state, it might be helpful to write down your thoughts as a letter to your teenager. The telephone can also be a great way to communicate. Not being in the same room, having the telephone as an intermediary, we once discovered, had a calming effect. Whatever method works best for you, the real challenge is to wait out those first anxious moments until composure returns.

   6. Always be direct and forthright. And finally there's one last route parents can take to open dialogue. *Be direct and forthright.* Don't just hint about your feelings. Come right out and say to your teenager, "I've got some real concerns. I know I may be stepping over the boundaries of your privacy, but I am your parent. If you listen to me about my concerns, I promise I will listen to you without overreacting or being overemotional."

   A straightforward approach often turns out to be the most effective way of opening up real communication between parent and child. We can try all sorts of devices, only to discover that what works best is just to "put the cards on the table."

The tough question:

7 | *"There is a real danger and unpleasantness in the world. How can I help my teenager face this reality without becoming cynical and pessimistic?"*

"It was so different when my kids were small. When something bad happened we covered up everything with sugar coating, pretended not to see, not to hear, and not to know. I remember one time when some older boys sneaked into our yard late one night and stuck glass on the slide. My son and daughter and their friends were badly cut. Why would anyone do this? We made believe it was an accident. No one could be as bad as to do something like that.

"We always did our best to shelter our kids. We made believe the world was all nice and pleasant and people weren't mean or evil. But we know there's more to life than make believe. How do I explain to my teenage son it wasn't unfair for him to be rejected by the college he so desperately wanted to attend?

"How do I tell my daughter that the teacher who didn't choose her for the cheerleading squad was wrong because she had a grudge against my daughter? We know some things in life aren't always just. When bad things happen to our kids, whose side do we take? When something hurts them, reality is like the shock of a glass of cold water in everyone's faces."

Mr. and Mrs. R., parents of three children,
twelve, fourteen, and seventeen

The tough answer:

How long can we shield our kids from some of life's harsh realities? As adults, we know only too well that life isn't always fair. Not all people are good; some people are evil; some people are going to cheat and lie; others will be honest. There's a lot of temptation to keep our kids sheltered from some of these all-too-true facts of life.

Our big child-rearing mistake was that we certainly tried to do this. We taught at a university. Before we began our careers, we had the idea that universities were sacred places, filled with people seeking wisdom. We thought that everyone would be idealistic, honest, and truthful. Outside one of the university buildings is a bronze statue of a seated man, chin in his hand. The name of the statue is "The Thinker" and that's how we imagined the faculty and students at this great institution would be. It was our dream to emulate these people we imagined to be so noble and contemplative.

It didn't take long for our innocence to be shattered. We discovered much to our dismay and shock that there were faculty and students who were inadequate, mean-spirited, dishonest, and, on occasion, downright evil. On the other hand, we also discovered there were plenty of individuals who came close to if not matched our ideal.

However, despite the fact that we discovered the reality of the institution, we tried not to think about it and went to great lengths to **make up** positive stories. And it was this set of myths that we communicated to our children. We didn't want to give up our idealistic fantasies, so we made sure we protected our kids and only selectively told them what really went on in some classrooms and with some of our colleagues.

Many years later we realize that we did them a great disservice. For example, when our teenage sons, on occasion, encountered manifestly unfair teachers we covered all this over with apologies and excuses. Thus, sometimes they saw themselves as wrong because we portrayed the teachers as always being right.

It isn't always easy to keep a balanced view of the harsher facts of life, and yet we now know that is *exactly* what a parent must do. For us to keep up the myth that *all* teachers are saintly people, always well intentioned, was wrong. What happens in such situations is that the youngster perceives himself as the one who is in error. It goes without saying that if the teacher is a perfect human being, when there is a problem it must be with the youngster.

The swimming coach who held a grudge against one son was terribly unfair. Just as the teacher who lauded his scientific accomplishments was fair and just. Parents have an obligation to help their kids sort out the facts of life. It isn't always easy, but parents can at least make an effort to keep a balanced viewpoint and, until the facts are in, avoid going overboard in either direction. We all know, only too well, that reality has many facets.

When your teenager comes home with a tale about unfairness of any sort, whether the unfairness involves other kids or the teachers, *listen*. That teacher he or she is complaining about may *indeed* be a problem, and it will be important for you to visit the school and find out for yourself what is going on.

There may be a group of youngsters with whom your child is having difficulties. Help your child find an acceptable solution to the problem.

It won't always be easy not to overreact. Keeping your feelings in check, sorting out the facts, and maintaining a balanced viewpoint are especially difficult because your emotions are involved. Everyone has to remember that there are plenty of rainbows in life—far more than rainfalls.

The tragic events of September 11, 2001, provide dramatic evidence that the world can be a dangerous place, and it would be unrealistic and unwise of parents to try to minimize the significance of what happened. Recognizing real dangers and learning to take realistic precautions, without unduly limiting normal activities, are crucial parts of growing up. It is therefore more important than ever that parents help their teenagers learn about these sad aspects of reality and at the same time provide the love, security, and reassurance that everyone needs in the process of becoming an adult.

The tough question:

8 | *"What should I do when my kids turn away from the church, challenge everything, and tell me the church has* no *meaning* in their lives?"*

"It was my daughter who started the rebellion. She tells me church has **no meaning in her life,** and would I please stop bugging her about religion. Her attitude, of course, has affected her brothers. She's the eldest, seventeen. The boys are twelve and fourteen. I could have predicted what they would say and what they would do because of her influence.

"For me, the church is very important. It's the rock, the foundation of morality. I look around at what's happening and, in my heart, I know more than ever how important a code of ethics, based on the church's teaching, is absolutely necessary to give life meaning.

"I don't want to lecture. It's my kids who bother me. Why are my kids fighting this? I have friends who have no problem. Their kids regularly attend Mass. I tell you I can't help but feel tremendous envy. What did they do right and what did we do wrong? My husband feels the same way. Both of us are upset."

Mr. and Mrs. Y., parents of two teenagers and one preteen

The tough answer:

Perhaps in an ideal world, Mr. and Mrs. Y.'s teenagers listen and follow their parents' suggestions without an argument or questioning. In the real world, this is not always the case. It's especially troublesome if we have friends whose children behave in ways we admire or think appropriate. Although we may be happy for our friends, let's never forget that jealousy is a *very normal and honest reaction.*

In answering this tough question about teenagers' rejection of church values or authority, our aim is to offer some suggestions that may help you get through this phase in your child's development without causing pain and dissension in your family or any family facing the same sort of problem.

By no means do we want to sound pompous or pretentious, but let's not any of us forget that religion is a complex matter. For the vast majority of adults, religion involves a pattern of rituals and morality unified by an underlying spiritual faith. And it's this spiritual faith that gives meaning to rituals and the moral beliefs of the church.

This kind of awareness ***doesn't automatically happen***. It takes a lot of living, a lot of experiences with life, whether it is birth, marriage, death, illness, or anything else, for a sense of faith beyond superficial behaviors to make sense.

Now, we might pause for a moment and think about religion from the perspective of teenagers. How can they possibly have these kinds of experiences? Why only a short time ago their concept of religion was, let's say, Christmas with presents and Santa Claus. Easter meant an Easter bunny and more presents. Suddenly they are teenagers. Religion doesn't carry with it the fun and games of early childhood. From their viewpoint the church seems to be primarily represented as a set of *do's and don'ts*, a collection of rules and rituals, without an embracing of the spiritual faith that gives these rules and rituals meaning. In one survey, we asked teenagers what religion meant to them. Rarely did youngsters respond with answers about spirituality. For most teenagers religion meant obeying specific rules such as not having sex before marriage, going to Mass regularly, saying prayers, going to confession.

Just as a small child views Christmas solely in terms of presents and the Santa Claus image, teenagers feel themselves hemmed in and bound by rules without tying then into a larger meaning of spiritual faith. It makes sense, doesn't it, that obedience is not going to be welcomed with open arms by a teenager?

Without a doubt, Mr. and Mrs. Y., we feel that your children's reaction against the church represents a generation gap. We don't believe that you should try to force behaviors. Furthermore, you should definitely avoid creating an emotional storm about religion. All you'll do is alienate your youngsters even more. For the moment, accept their negative feelings.

Remember yourselves as teenagers. Were you happy with a lot of controls over your behavior? Were you delighted about having to obey rules you felt didn't make sense? We urge you to use the teenagers turning away from the church as a chance for *dialogue*. How else can they acquire a sense that there's something more than just a simple "no" unless you provide some guidance about a greater, more profound meaning to your faith? Don't forget this is *not* a teaching situation, but rather a chance for you to express your feelings about what faith means to you.

However, let's say your efforts fail. There are still other things you might do to encourage religious interest. Teenage years are a time of socialization. There's a strong pull to be with one's peers. Thus, anything you can do to encourage involvement in church activities, even if they are *primarily social*, should be a top priority. Don't worry unduly about whether your teenager goes to Mass. Rather, focus on whether your youngster attends, for example, a church-sponsored party at holiday time. Just being in the right atmosphere can be important.

We honestly feel that belief in religious values, that is one's faith, is developmental. Recognizing this can go a long way toward easing tensions within a family when a teenager starts actively rejecting faith. Just as you would not have expected your six-year-old to think of much else other than what presents the Easter bunny was going to deliver to his door, don't push at the teenager and expect your sixteen-year-old to feel inner piety, holiness, or spiritual faith when his or her own thoughts are on an upcoming soccer game or the junior prom. Be realistic in your expectations of what is appropriate for the age.

Let time and maturity take their course. Someday your teenager will have the requisite learning experiences to receive the *gift of faith*. By all means do whatever you can through your own behavior, through positive encouragement, but allow time for your youngster to reach a point in life when the church can be viewed not as a set of prohibitions but as an avenue through which to find and shape his or her own spirituality.

Just never forget that if you make it an issue, religion is going to become a focus for conflict. You don't want this kind of battleground. There are no winners—only losers. Sometimes in trying to effect changes in your teenager's attitudes or behavior, the waiting game and patience can be nerve-racking. It's hard to believe that the future will be different. However, we have found that parents can be helped, as we were, with a big dose of empathy for their teenagers. For example, often when we would get into one of these no-win dialogues, going around in circles, we would remember our behavior as teenagers. Holding up this kind of mirror can go a long way toward reducing tensions!

The tough question:

9 | *"How can I best help my teenager fulfill his/her own potential without creating too much pressure?"*

"I feel terribly conflicted. On the one hand, I think I should just sit back and let my son and daughter go off and do their own thing. By this, however, I mean give them opportunities. How and what they do with these opportunities is their decision, *not* mine. On the other hand, it drives me up a wall when I see talents in my son that are being wasted. He has so many skills.

"My daughter, too. I have this awful feeling they are drifting, wasting their time. One day it's science, the next day music, and the next week they're ready to chuck everything. It's all fine and good when so-called experts talk about not overdoing direction, parental pressure, and demands, but, let's face it, this is not the same world as it was years ago. Kids need to develop skills in this day and age."

Mrs. O., mother of three teenagers

"Every now and then I read or hear about parents and their kids and how the kids follow the parents' lead and go off to become skating stars, famous scientists, or whatever. Parents guided, even pushed those kids. No rebellion; no resistance. The kids even say they owe their success to their parents. My wife and I have friends we think are doing all the wrong things. They're always after their kids about doing well in school. And you know what? Their kids are great students, superperformers. They don't seem bothered in the least by parental pressure. We would give anything to know their magic formula.

"There's a lot of competition out there. There are expectations, financial pressure. Kids who sit back and do nothing with their teenage years are going to be left out of the future. They're going to be at a disadvantage if they don't get their act together early in life. We want our kids to be successful. We just never seem to know what is the difference between encouragement and pushing. It's just not so simple to stay our of our kids' lives, not to take an active interest."

Mr. R., father of two teenagers,
a fourteen-year-old boy and
a sixteen-year-old girl

The tough answer:

Being encouraging without being demanding, showing interest without demonstrating concern, being helpful without exerting pressure—sometimes we're convinced the role of a parent is one exercise after another in behavioral and emotional gymnastics. When we were psychology graduate students, we thought we understood the complexities of what it meant to be a parent. Certainly the right and wrong methods were made abundantly clear in the research literature.

Of course, at that time in our lives, it was easy for us to be experts about the subject. *We didn't as yet have children.* The crucial difference in our thinking came *after* our children became teenagers. It took us years of muddling through our own problems in child-rearing as well as studying other families to finally come up with some principles of raising children that not only made sense but had the potential of making an enormous difference in the overall relationship of parents and teenagers.

Unfortunately, by the time we sorted out this wisdom, our sons were out of their teens and well into adulthood. Our only hope, or so we rationalized, was that the knowledge acquired from early mistakes would help us in relating to them as adults. We think that is the case. However, all we do know is that we're far better in the grandparenting role.

Experts are always cautioning against overparenting. The advice given to parents is to back off; stay uninvolved, don't jump in and try to solve your child's problems; let a youngster mature at his or her own pace. Objectively, this makes sense. All this advice is great when it refers to someone else's child. However, what most authorities forget to take into account is the *emotional component* or how parents feel.

One father told us that it broke his heart to see his daughter pulling Cs and Ds in high school, threatening her chances of getting into a good college. "Until her teen years she was a whiz, a fireball. It's all changed. Every time one of those report cards with warnings comes home, I want to blow my top, take away every privilege. How would you feel?"

Our reply is, "horrible." We think most parents would feel devastated. Turning away, keeping one's silence just isn't that simple when it comes to relating to your own child. Thus, whatever advice you choose to follow, just don't forget that the emotional factor is important to consider.

You're going to have to walk a tightrope sometimes to keep your feelings in control. But let's backtrack a bit and recount an experience in our own lives that has provided us with a number of important insights about how to best develop a child's potential while avoiding pressure.

Joel was a good tennis player. He enjoyed the game and played high school and college tennis. I was also involved in tennis. Before our children could walk, they were quite accustomed to sitting in baby carriages on the side of the tennis courts, wearing mini-tennis hats and tennis outfits for pretoddlers. While we played other sports, there was no question about the family interest in tennis. Twice a year, for the U.S. Open and Wimbledon, we were glued to the television set.

As soon as they could walk, each boy had a tennis racket and with the helpful, concerned guidance of their parents they were taken out to the tennis courts and applauded every time they hit the ball. Of course, we didn't want to *falsely* encourage them, so there were *plenty of times we were less than positive*. We prefer not to talk about those sessions, which later on left one boy in tears, and the other unnerved.

When they were in their teens we repeatedly emphasized that we didn't want champions. Tennis, we assured them, was a great sport. We rationalized our encouragement by telling each other that, if the boys had not been naturally athletic or did not possess great skill and superb coordination, we would never dream of pushing them to play.

Remember, we are psychologists. We knew it was unwise to push. On the other hand, it seemed such a waste to sit back and do nothing in the face of all this talent. We weren't pushing, we told ourselves, we were merely encouraging.

Did we feel twinges of excitement at seeing some development? You can rest assured we did. We believed that they, too, would play college tennis, perhaps win scholarships. They, too, would go far beyond their parents' modest success. Nearly every parent we have surveyed has shared "secret" hopes about their children's future.

To make sure we weren't overdoing our concern we would always say such things as, "Just do your best. We don't want you to go to Wimbledon. We don't really think about the U.S. Open. It doesn't matter if someday you don't play on the high school or college team."

We thought our choice of words was perfect. In retrospect, we would like to be fair to ourselves. At the time we were totally unaware, even with all our psychological sophistication, that we might have been sending double messages. We *thought* we were saying what we really believed. We didn't want great champions.

They, on the other hand, heard another implicit message. "Yes, we would like you to go to Wimbledon. We would like you to go to the U.S. Open. We would like you to play top high school and college tennis." If someone had told us that was the real message we were communicating, we would have been very angry. Us? Send out contrary signals? Remember, we saw ourselves as wise psychologists, all too familiar with the dangers of overparenting.

Any signs that everything wasn't going along as we planned were ignored. A very furious argument about tennis was smoothed over with a new racket, the offer of the use of a family car, extra presents. Our reasoning was that if we rewarded them with praise we would achieve our desire to make them into good players.

And now it is time to tell you about one lovely spring afternoon, a perfect tennis day that was not too warm, not too hot. The boys had **great, new, expensive rackets.** We even told them that, when we were their age, our parents couldn't afford to buy us rackets costing as much as theirs did. (Just a little more pressure.) Of course, our expectations were that they would be thrilled with such special presents.

It isn't necessary to go into all the details of the afternoon's trauma. You will get the idea about what happened when we tell you that one racket, flung against the steel fence, lay twisted on the ground. The other racket disappeared into the bottom of a pond adjoining the public town court area.

Two vows were made. One son swore he would **never** touch a tennis racket again. He has kept his word. The other son, also an athlete, never competed or played tennis in high school or in college.

It was totally without awareness that we placed so much emphasis on tennis. Only now, in retrospect, are we grateful and fortunate that our **helpful** guidance did not extend into other facets of their lives. Luckily, we were pretty single-minded; otherwise, we shudder to think of the consequences of the same kind of pressure, for example, on their academic performance.

In telling this story, we want readers to keep in mind that if you had seen them on a tennis court as young teenagers, you would understand how difficult it was for us to remain silent. At the time, given our personal interest in the game, and their talent, we could see nothing amiss with what we were doing. How wrong we were!

What we totally forgot is that every teenager is unique. What works best for any given child or parent may be completely inappropriate for another teenager. You will have to judge your particular circumstances. However, despite all the enormous individual differences, we have some important suggestions in answer to the tough question about how parents can best help a youngster achieve or fulfill his/her potential without creating too much pressure.

1. Parents have to be careful not to project their own goals onto their children. How easy this is to do. If you thought of becoming a great scientist and were a bit short of achieving this dream, and you have a child who is a scientifically gifted teenager, it's very tempting to push just a little bit and then a little bit more. Just remember that this dream is *your* dream and not necessarily your teenager's. In our family, we call the separate world of parent-child dreams "the Wimbledon complex."

2. It's important to provide opportunities for teenagers to pursue and develop their own talents. How and what you do as teacher is a very "touchy" subject. We taught other people's children for decades; however, we discovered that we were totally ineffective when it came to trying to directly teach our own kids anything. It wasn't for a lack of interest on our part, but emotional stumbling blocks doomed our efforts.

Of course, you may be fortunate and won't have problems. However, for *most* of us, parent-child rivalries, overconcern, and intensity can get in the way of learning. Just remember this and step back from getting involved in your child's life as a teacher when you see warning signs that your efforts are not making anyone in the family happy.

3. Be an appreciative audience. Reward but do not buy performance. Trying to give bribes or rewards such as increased allowance, a special tennis racket, and unusual gifts of any sort to gain certain ends will not have any long-term effect. In fact, the opposite may occur. The teenager will be resentful or retreat. What really will make a difference in whether or not teenagers pursue a goal is the *intrinsic reward of the activity.*

What they do has to matter to *them*, make a difference in the way they feel about *themselves*. This doesn't mean that you bend over backward not to reward, but don't use a special reward or gift as a bargaining wedge. There won't be any lasting effects. You might "buy" an A grade once, but the next time around there can be a slipping into old habits unless the activity or what was accomplished made an impression on their own egos.

4. Watch out for signs of trouble regarding pressure. We should have recognized what was happening when we watched one tennis match and saw our son wildly hitting balls he never would have missed unless he felt uncomfortable, competitive pressure. If your teenager enjoys competition, whether it is in academics or sports, be sure you don't step over the line and become involved in any way. The decision to be competitive must come from the teenager, not your desire for a winner.

5. Try not to fall into an evaluative mode. When the grade is not the greatest or the performance is not super, hold back on judgments. "You can do a lot better if only you would try," said to a teenager with a less-than-great grade in a subject can induce a lot of tension. By the same token expressing great disappointment can only induce guilt. Just be straightforward about your feelings. Don't mask with false compliments; don't overdo criticism if you are unhappy.

6. Help your teenager be realistic about goals. Although we've focused on parents and teenage pressures, there are lots of other people who may try to influence your child's life. Even if these individuals are well-intentioned they can cause problems.

We remember one son's guitar teacher. Our teenager plucked away rather nicely. At least his friends were appreciative. An overeager teacher kept encouraging him, and with misguided judgment thought that by offering some classical pieces as a big challenge our son would be motivated to really excel.

He was given several impressive works to master. The music was way beyond his ability. As a result, lesson after lesson ended with him feeling hopeless. The teacher's error did a great deal toward shortening that son's desire to continue playing the instrument either alone or with his buddies.

Learning to be realistic about one's abilities is extremely important and this is where parents can be helpful. ***Don't push*** and ***don't overplay*** should be your watchwords. But it is also important to make sure that the outside world doesn't make mistakes. Teachers other than yourself or well-meaning family members can carry praise just too far. If success is not attained, the fall can be truly harmful.

7. Never, never compare your adolescent to other adolescents or to yourself as a teenager. We remember only too well visiting friends who showed us the basement of their home. Their teenage son had built a high-fidelity set. In another corner was a fully equipped darkroom where the youngster developed and printed film. He already had a successful business going.

Our admiration was unreserved. In our house, we paid for film to be developed and any audio equipment we bought had to be assembled by the store. At the dinner table that evening everyone talked about the other boy's accomplishments. We thought that we were just honestly praising.

Our son had agreed that his friend had marvelous mechanical and engineering skills. We must have said something about why he didn't try doing some of these kinds of things. I guess fantasies of the money we could save with "do-it-yourself" projects were in the back of our minds. Our son was silent. He flung down his fork, got up from the table and quietly said to us, "Do you feel stuck with me?"

Without conscious awareness we had slipped into that most unfortunate of child-rearing errors, *parenting-by-comparison*. We were making him feel inferior through comparison. If our goal was to have him build a high-fidelity set, we should have come right out and made the suggestion rather than beat around the bush. Our compliments for the other teenager implied indirect criticism of our son.

And last but not least, avoid reminiscing at length about your virtues and success at the same age. No teenager responds with warmth and enthusiasm to a parental lecture that begins with a raised finger and a strong voice, "when I was your age..." followed by a listing of accomplishments.

8. Do whatever you can to encourage your adolescent to discover his or her own particular talents and to set achievement goals that fit these talents. Just never forget that the talents your youngster possesses may be vastly different from your own. Moreover, it's important to remember that not everyone is going to excel in every way. Learn to value the particular talents your child has without trying to impose your own ideals.

We believe that every teenager has a right to determine which of his talents provides him with the greatest pleasure. Teenage years are inevitably going to include failures, defeats, and frustrations that may seem inappropriate from an adult's perspective. But it is only through such experience that adolescents honestly discover what they are good at and what they are not so good at—what they find challenging, enjoyable, and self-fulfilling and what they find dull, dreary, and uninteresting.

Meaningful achievement can mean a variety of things, not only an A in a course or a big win in a sport. Regardless of what your adolescent's achievements are, pay attention to them. Appreciate individual skills and talents. *Listen more than talk; encourage more than direct; inform but don't evaluate.*

"How am I doing?" asks the adolescent.

"How do you think you're doing? Are you satisfied, happy, proud of yourself? That's what really matters," should be the parental reply.

The tough question:

10 | *"Sex, drugs, alcohol— the three big concerns. What can I do?"*

"Two of the girls who came to my daughter's sweet-sixteen party were pregnant. I had no idea. When they walked in, I was shocked. I think my daughter had been afraid to tell me. Friends helping me with the luncheon told me later that they thought they were going to have to pick me up off the floor.

"Of course, I was upset. What if this had been my daughter? It's every mother's nightmare, I can tell you. I couldn't even bring myself to talk about it with her. I thought if I said anything it would be so horrible she would get angry. I didn't have to spoil her birthday. Even now as I talk about it I feel the same tension as I did a month ago.

"Let me say, too, what still upsets me is the fact the girls at the party all accepted everything like it was OK. If this had happened to me or any of my friends when I was the same age, there would have been hell to pay. What is happening nowadays? Am I as a parent not seeing something?"

Mrs. J., mother of a sixteen-year-old girl

"A kid down the street wrapped his family car around a tree. It happened a couple of weeks ago. Someone was watching over him, that's for sure. Evidently, he stumbled out of the car without a scratch. The kids had been drinking beer. Now it's a joke with some of my son's friends, 'Big deal, smart-ass kid made it through.' If anyone else had been in the car they wouldn't be here now; we'd be going to funerals.

"I know I can't hold my son's hand. I can't go out on Saturday night with the guys and sit there monitoring what he does. All I can do is worry now when he takes the car on weekends. I talk myself blue in the face. 'Don't drink, damn it. You can kill yourself.' How do I know he's listening?"

Father of a teenage boy

"We moved to the suburbs because we wanted out from the city and problems. It was all so nice in the beginning when the kids were small. But I'm finding out that suburbia doesn't mean escape from problems. My kids are teenagers and their world is all upside down from the world I knew at the same age.

"This past year one of the boys in the neighborhood died from an overdose. None of us had any idea he was on drugs. He seemed like a nice kid. I remember him sitting in our kitchen having hot chocolate. The boys had been playing hockey. The absurdity of it—hot chocolate and a couple of weeks later we're going to a wake.

"If there was only one kid, then maybe we could all rationalize. But it isn't one. Our son's school faculty has admitted there's a drug problem. My husband and I feel like we're on some high wire shaking with fear."

Mother of a teenage boy

The tough answer:

These aren't rare anecdotes reported for shock value. We are absolutely certain that each of you could cite your own stories about pregnant teenagers and drug and alcohol abuse. When we queried parents about problems by asking them to list their major concerns, alcohol, drug abuse, and sexual activity frequently appeared as big concerns.

This makes sense. As one parent commented, "If my son buckles under pressure, flunks a test, it isn't the end of the world. There's always another chance. A kid fooling around with drugs, alcohol, or sex may not have that second chance." The threat of irreparable physical, moral, and spiritual damage is all too real.

Parents can't sit back with a "wait and see" attitude. They can't just hope for a turnaround. They can't bide their time thinking the teenager will grow up and out of bad habits. *Active parenting is an absolute must.* Throughout this book, we've always stressed the importance of dialogue, open communication, listening to the teenager, empathizing with the teenager, and above all treating the teenager like a colleague, a good friend, and an adult.

We aren't qualifying these suggestions with respect to the subjects we have thus far discussed. However, when it comes to sex, drugs, and alcohol, parents have to take a firm, decisive stance. An important part of parenting teenagers involves helping kids gain some *impulse control.* When a child is small and demands a chocolate ice cream immediately, parents may give in with some amusement at the fierce determination of a toddler's manner. After all, there's nothing life-threatening in the desire.

However, where the "big three" are concerned, parents can't backtrack on their position. They have an obligation to their kids (and, frankly, to themselves) to take a firm, uncompromising position. The possibilities for self-destruction are far too great to risk any kind of softened approach.

Thus, in response to the question "How does one cope?" our reply is that parents must cope by *directly* facing each of these issues. Don't hope the problem will go away. Don't depend on outsiders, teachers, counselors, or anyone else to do your job. More than ever, this is a time for honesty. The subjects may make you uncomfortable, but teenagers will have a healthy respect for a parent who comes out and says, "Talking about sex makes me uncomfortable. I find it hard because when I was growing up such discussions didn't go on at home or in school, but this is the twenty-first century."

Teenagers who told us their parents were able to talk about everything in the world except for sex admitted they were stunned when their parents tried this direct approach. Parents have to use their own words, of course, but the loud and clear message should be the importance of sex in a mature adult marriage and the risks psychologically, morally, and physically when sex occurs at an inappropriate time in the youngster's life.

The same forthright approach has to be used with drugs and alcohol. There can be no bargaining and no compromising. Parents have to be strong and sure in their position regarding these matters. The safety and welfare of one's child is central in life.

We do also feel that kids deserve a *full* explanation about why parents are taking such a strong position. Of course, the safety and welfare of the teenager are important, but we also think this is the time for parents to make sure their teenager understands that the limits parents seek to impose on their child's behavior stem *not* from anger but from love.

This is not easy for a teenager to appreciate. We all know that when we lecture teenagers we're apt to say something like, "This is for your own good. You play with fire like drugs and you can get burned. If you have sex before marriage, you are not only committing a sin but you run the risk of ruining something that can be truly meaningful between you and a spouse when the time is right." While these parental comments are undoubtedly true, they may very well fall on the deaf ears of our teenagers if we do not at the same time communicate love and genuine concern.

With little children we show love through touching, holding, cuddling, and kissing. These physical acts drop off as kids get older. With some teenagers, a hug can be embarrassing. We aren't likely to cuddle teenagers. Thus, without the same physical contact, all we have left are words. And when parents are in the lecturing mode, words such as, "We love you very much," may not ring with a great deal of emotional force when you first try to communicate your feelings.

However, in any way that is comfortable, parents have an obligation to let the teenager know that every bit of their concern stems from love, and love that binds a parent to a child is very special. Give yourself a chance to deal with these problems. However, if your suspicions are true and you have a teenager who needs more guidance than you, a parent, can provide, don't wait. Seek outside help immediately. Don't wait before it's too late!

The tough question:

11 | *"What do I do when I get into an argument with my teenager?"*

"It doesn't take much to set either of us off. That bothers me. I'll make an innocent comment. My son reacts, and then I react to him. Off we go at each other's throats. I finally asked him, 'Why can't we ever talk like human beings? Why do we always have to end up fighting with each other about silly things?'

"He insists it's not him. I disagree. I know sometimes in the heat of an argument we say things to each other that are just horrible. He doesn't mind, or at least it seems like that. After these tiffs, I'm the one who stays awake. I feel sad, hurt, and then I get angrier at him because I think it's his fault that I behave the way I do."

Mrs. W., mother of a teenage son

"I have the feeling," one father told us, "sometimes my son just itches for a battle. He'll go out of his way to provoke me. He knows what buttons to press until I finally explode. What is this with kids? I get this feeling my son wants to fight with me for the pure devil of it."

"I thought it was just boys who got a kick of trying to get a rise out of me and make me lose my temper," said one mother. "But was I in for a surprise when my daughter became a teenager. She's no different from her brothers. She'll stand in the kitchen while I am making dinner and say things both of us know are going to upset me. One time she told me she was going to a party and all the boys and girls were planning to stay overnight. Of course, I was bothered. I told her I didn't think it was a good idea since she didn't even know where this party was going to be held.

"Well, that did it. According to her, I didn't trust her. I didn't believe she was going to stay out of trouble. In my eyes she was a baby. Because of my dumb Victorian attitude she was going to end up friendless. Obviously, the argument skyrocketed. We didn't speak for three days."

The tough answer:

Teenage years without verbal conflicts? Unlikely. At one time or another (and hopefully it won't be frequently), every parent is bound to get into an argument with a teenager. One can only hope, as we did, that these battles don't deteriorate into actual physical combat. We assure you there were moments when this almost was the case.

The substance of many arguments with teenagers often isn't very earthshaking. In fact, if there is a real problem, a dramatic crisis, parents and teenagers can and do become allies. Perhaps in those situations the problem is so overwhelming that both sides realize how pointless it would be to prolong the fighting.

What is interesting is how arguments beginning with something very minor frequently escalate into major issues. This is exactly what happened with John, fifteen-years-old, and his mother. We asked him how the fight began.

"With the lawnmower." (Lawn mowing or any other household chore is not an uncommon source of teenage-parent squabbling.) "What did your mother say?"

"She was angry because I hadn't mowed the lawn."

"Was that your job?"

"Yes."

"Had you done your job?"

"No."

"For how long?"

"Three weeks."

From that point on John's mother expressed her outrage at his laziness. The tirade went back and forth.

Although the hostile words began with failure to mow the lawn, they ended with John's failure to apologize for his general inattention to responsibilities, his lack of respect for his parents who both worked, and their resentment at providing him with food, shelter, and clothing without asking very much in return except for simple acts such as mowing the lawn. Finally, they compared John's behavior with a neighbor's angelic son who not only mowed the lawn and cut the shrubs, but regularly took out the trash.

Given the stepped-up attack, it is not any mystery that John and his mother ended up feeling bitter toward each other. His mother had accused him of being lazy, which wounded his vanity. He, on the other hand, had used some expletives, which, he realized in a more rational moment, would have been better left unsaid.

Arguments have a way of spiraling. They may begin with inconsequential specifics and end with everything the teenager or parent has done for the past dozen or so years that is perceived as wrong.

Janice, seventeen, described a recent battle she had with her father. A friend of hers was over at the house on a Saturday afternoon and came up to her room.

"We had the door open. He sat on my bed. I wanted to show him my report. My father happened to come by. He saw the two of us. He didn't say anything right there. I would have died if he had insulted me or my friend. Later, after Rich left, Dad demanded to know what was going on.

"I told him about the report. He lectured to me for hours. He said that he was hurt and disappointed. I was to be grounded. I asked for what. He couldn't come right out and say it, but I knew what he was hinting at. I told him to say it. He said he'd be damned if he would.

"I told him he was trying to imply we were having sex.

"He denied this, but I know that was on his mind. So it got worse and worse. I told him, if I had been having sex, I certainly wouldn't have left the door open."

"So you were having sex."

"I told him that was ridiculous. I just said that because he was making me so angry.

"Anyhow, he said he wasn't going to allow me to have any more dates. If I didn't like the house rules, I could go live elsewhere. I couldn't believe this. All I had done was have this friend, and he isn't even a boyfriend, up to my room because my kid brothers were raising hell downstairs. Rich is an A student and I really wanted him to look at my report."

Although in our house we did our best to try to avoid fights, bent over backward to be reasonable, there were times when conflicts arose. We have never known parents who haven't at one time or another locked horns with their teenagers. Different opinions and disagreements make psychological sense. After all, the teenager is growing up, searching for independence and ready to break loose from parental controls, ready to think and to make judgments that may radically differ from those of the parents.

But why the need, on occasion, to turn differences of opinion into a battleground? It is our belief that the underlying reason for arguments getting out of hand is because of a power struggle. Parents are reluctant to give in to their teenager. Teenagers dig their heels in and refuse to give in to parents' authority.

There's an impasse that someone has to break, and we think this has to be the parents. But first we want to emphasize that, in battle with a teenager, there are no winners—only losers. The losers will be you, the parents.

When we made this point with a number of parents, their first reaction was clearly irritation and disbelief. What do we mean by parents being losers? Parents provide financial support. They have judgment and should be deferred to by their children. Children must respect parents' authority.

This kind of thinking won't be of much help in resolving conflicts with a teenager. First of all, both the parent and the teenager see the conflict as a contest, a battle, and all battles have winners and losers. While the parent may win in the sense that the teenager sullenly retreats or hangs his or her head in shame or suffers other indignities, the ***psychological wounds never heal.*** We're taking a long-range view. What are really important are the long-term effects. What happens in a relationship in the teen years is an important foundation for the relationship between parents and their children years in the future.

The challenge is to look at the whole process of resolving conflicts with teenagers with a completely new perspective. Try not to see the differences as conflicts with prosecuting attorneys and defendants. For example, the mother's goal in the lawnmower case may be a determination to prove that the teenager is lazy, irresponsible, thoughtless, and entirely to blame for the unsightly grass around the house.

In rebuttal, the teenager may view her as unfair, narrow-minded, old-fashioned, and indifferent to his other responsibilities or activities. Besides, what is so god-awful about uncut grass?

Each of the combatants goes around and around, doing their very best to assign blame to each other. Wrapped up in his or her own arguments, the other person is rarely heard, much less understood. The basic difficulty with this approach is that the aim of both parent and adolescent assigning blame to the other person is largely irrelevant to solving whatever problem has arisen. As long as that mutual aim of assigning blame remains, little can be accomplished.

To short circuit this vicious cycle of blame and counterblame, one person needs to realize that whenever there is a problem between parent and adolescent, both inevitably contribute to the discussion. Thus, the sooner parents and teenagers stop playing the "blame game" with each other, the sooner they can make an effort toward mutual understanding and the quicker they will find a resolution to their troubles.

When disagreements arise between you and your adolescent, don't get caught in the trap of assigning blame. Remember that you are the parent, not a prosecuting attorney, and nothing gets resolved by proving your adolescent guilty.

We feel that parents are in a better position to stop the cycle and break the impasse not because they have a more secure position or greater power. Rather, their strength lies *only* in their ability to more readily shift their focus from assigning blame to gaining mutual understanding because they are older and wiser.

As long as a parent keeps talking, even if the talking is argumentative, there is a chance of breaking through to some reasonable solution. A fight can be painful, but at least then they are in some sort of contact with each other. A much more devastating problem occurs when parent and adolescent withdraw from each other and communication breaks down completely. Living in a home with sullen silence is not pleasant for anyone.

Thus, anything you as a parent can do to keep communication lines open is critical. Express your feelings by all means. Just remember to make sure to express your feelings from your point of view without one hint of attack or prosecution. And then give your teenager his or her turn. **Be a willing, loving listener**.

We do not mean to imply that merely talking to each other automatically leads to a resolution of problems that develop between parents and teenagers. Obviously, talk is merely a medium for exchanging ideas, opinions, and information, and sharing feelings, values, and experiences. However, it is *only* through this exchange and sharing that resolution can be achieved.

A problem for many parents, including ourselves, stems from what we believe may possibly be a false sense of parental prerogative. We may feel hurt and insulted by comments teenagers make in the course of their battles; as a result, parents refuse to continue talking until their teenagers apologize, give in, or in some way demonstrate respect for their parents' status and position.

In most cases, apology is the last thing on the teenager's mind, and the situation rapidly deteriorates. The parent feels bitter and hurt by the teenager's disrespect and the teenager feels more angry and frustrated. Parents must recognize that it is really not a matter of respect or disrespect. Persistent focus on the issue of whether or not their teenagers have shown proper respect for their parents will only make the situation progressively worse, not better.

This lesson is crucial: Don't focus on the issue of proper respect, an idea that very early gets in the way of dealing effectively with the more significant problems that arise in relations between parents and adolescents. *Instead, concentrate your efforts on continuing to keep open the communication channels between you and your teenager.* Stop playing the blame game. Be the first to break the vicious cycle of attack and defense by stopping your attacks, making defense unnecessary, and working toward mutual empathic understanding.

To achieve this goal, keep the following in mind:

● *Use "I" messages to express your opinions and feelings as clearly as you can.*
  Suppose your teenager comes home late. If you greet him or her at the door with an accusing "You're late," it's quite likely that your teenager will feel attacked and become defensive. Instead, you might focus on your own feelings, with a state-

ment such as, "I was worried" or "I was concerned about you." Thus, you are simply expressing your own feeling, rather than accusing or attacking and your teenager is less likely to respond defensively or hostilely.

- *Stay focused on the problem. Don't generalize about other issues.*

- *Recognize that people can disagree and still live together with genuine affection and respect.*

- *Work out realistic compromises!*
  Don't let conventional signs of proper respect get in the way of your search for mutual understanding. After the storm is over, be the *first* to take that important step of forgiveness: a hug and a kiss, an arm around a son or daughter's shoulder. We have never regretted the times when we have said to our teenagers, "We're sorry. We, too, make mistakes." When our teenagers and we heard this kind of message, we could then move on in a relationship that became stronger and more bonded. We truly believe that our having done this at critical points in their teenage years was a giant step toward helping our sons learn what is meant by mutual respect and understanding; not only in the family, but in their relationships in the outside world.

The tough question:

12 | *"What do I do about my teenager's mood swings?"*

"One minute he's on top of the world; the next minute he locks himself in his room, turns up the stereo, blasting it loud enough to make us all deaf. You can't get a word out of him. As a little boy he was always sunshine. Now there are days when all I do is look at him, say, 'Hi, how's everything?' only to have him accusing me of nagging, not letting him have any privacy.

"I can see that look on his face. I once said to him, 'How about a smile once in a while. It's not the end of the world.'

"And he snapped back, 'In whose opinion?'

"Everyone has off moments. We're human. What bothers me is the unpredictability of his moods. The swings are getting to us. Sure, he has good days. We get smiles, hugs, but a lot of the time it seems life is an emotional roller coaster."

Mrs. O., mother of a seventeen-year-old boy

The tough answer:

Shoulders slouched, no eye contact, maybe a smirk; corners of the mouth turned down, hands in pockets; stereo blasting; television set turned up full volume; the front door slamming so hard one can just imagine it snapping off of its hinges. Parents cringe. It's pretty obvious their teenager is moving into one of those inevitable, moody, teenage blue periods.

And then, of course, there is the contrasting side. The teenager's step is light and carefree; there are smiles, exciting expansive plans. "How was your day?" a parent asks.

"Terrific," is the response. "Maybe I'll clean up my room."

A whistled song, stereo played at an acceptable volume, and parents breathe a sigh of relief. The teenager is on the upswing. Life is great. *Maybe having kids was a good idea after all.*

Are mood swings inevitable? Probably so. It's unlikely that a teenager can sail through growing up years without some dramatic mood changes. Knowing that mercurial behavior has a psychological basis can be very helpful in learning how to deal with moods. The first important step is for parents to accept the swings with understanding, and, above all, to make sure they keep a clear head and not let themselves get caught up on the same emotional roller coaster.

"Up" periods usually offer no problems, other than trying to tone down the excitement of perhaps some unrealistic plans. However, it isn't all so easy when the dark or low side moves in. It's tough on parents not to overreact. We think back with regret to one time when our son had a fight with a swim coach. The coach, a vindictive person in our opinion, decided that our son could not be nominated to be captain of the swim team. He was angry and hurt, but we aren't sure whether his anger or disappointment could possibly have matched the hurt we felt for him.

Empathy worsened the situation. We could not think rationally; our emotions ran rampant. Over time, he resolved the problem in his own way, and triumphed in another sport. He made his point, achieved a victory.

What could we have done? We certainly could have avoided intensifying the problem by sharing our feelings. *Listen with an extra measure of sympathy and understanding*. In this situation, we became so caught up in the turmoil of the moment we couldn't think clearly. Our involvement perhaps made the unpleasantness last a lot longer than it should have.

In no way are we saying you should never intervene. There will be times for the safety, welfare, and mental health of your teenager that intervention is an *absolute must*. Just count to ten before you take action.

Sometimes when you're still all upset, you may discover that your teenager is once again "happy as a lark." There are occasions when parents have stepped in and gotten all worked up only to discover that, while they are still simmering, the teenager has completely forgotten what the fuss was about. We think it's not unlike the old game of "pass the hot potato." The adolescent "dumps" all his agony and stress onto a parent. Free from the emotional burden, the teenager can get on with his or her life.

Parents of one teenage girl reported just such an experience. For several months their lives were agony. Their daughter had not been invited to the prom. "I can't tell you how many nights my husband and I sat there wondering what to do, how we could soothe over her bitter disappointment. Not going to the prom for our daughter was a major tragedy. We may minimize its importance, but when you're sixteen it especially hurts when all your friends are supposedly going.

"One night I stood outside her bedroom door. I was sure I heard her crying. I knocked; She told me she wanted to be alone. I thought I was going to get an ulcer from the anxiety. Any number of times I brought up the subject and tried to make her feel better. We would end up having words, with her telling me I had no idea how she felt, which wasn't true. The tension was getting to all of us.

"Finally, I decided we'd go to a movie the night of the prom. First, we would go out to dinner. I would get her a new outfit. My plan included everything to make up for the disappointment of the prom. All I told her was that we were planning something special, and I mentioned the date.

"She looked surprised.

"'Can't. Other plans. I must have forgotten to tell you. Tommy asked me to the prom. He's kind of neat.'"

The parents later admitted that their tension had made matters worse. Not only did their daughter have to contend with her own concerns, but also she was only too aware of her mother and father's anxiety about the prom.

Living from one crisis to another in the teenage years is a big mistake, not only for the parents but also for what it does to the teenager. Sometimes it is better for everyone involved to "cool it." Let the tensions have time to simmer down and fade away.

The tough question:

13 | *"How can I best prepare my teenager to be independent of the family?"*

"We've been so close in our family. I know lots of families where the kids can't wait to get out of the house and be on their own. That isn't the case with us. My kids like their home—maybe too much. My husband says that we better not make everything so comfortable around here or they'll never want to leave.

"I realize I still look at them as my kids. I don't quite see them as adults, and yet I know they've got to have some preparation for a time when they will be leaving home. Kids should not stay tied to the apron strings long after they should be doing their own thing, but that's a lot easier to say than do!"

Mother of three teenagers

The tough answer:

In *Peter Pan*, the little boys stay small children in spirit and mind. They don't grow up. There is something endearing about small kids: playfulness, charm, innocence, and excitement at discovering the world. And then suddenly they are tall enough so that we look straight into their eyes instead of downward to meet their gaze. Little kids grow up in stature. It's something we would never dream of preventing, but rather actively encourage. However, it's something some parents find difficult to do with respect to everything else in their child's life.

Letting our kids grow up means pulling back a bit in every aspect of their lives while still keeping a watchful eye. It does take a lot of balancing of priorities. The danger of not easing youngsters into independence as soon as they reach the teenage years does them a disservice.

We can think of no better example than Nicole's father, who had all sorts of rules about the age he was going to allow his daughter to go out with boys.

The idea of twelve- and thirteen-year-olds hanging out with boys was disturbing to Mr. C. "I don't understand how parents let their daughter in situations that pose some risks. When she's old enough, then, of course, I'll let her date like any normal girl."

In his opinion sixteen years of age was about right for her to attend boy-girl affairs and to go out socially with boys. We spoke with Nicole. All her friends were going to boy-girl parties and some were having single dates. Nicole felt left outside of the loop of her friends.

"That's fine," said her father, "let her feel left out. I told her when the time comes she can join the other kids. Hopefully, by that time she'll be able to judge what is acceptable and what is not."

Our contention is that the longer he holds back and prevents Nicole from having much social contact before the magic age of sixteen, the harder it will be for her. Learning independence is cumulative. One isn't dependent and then overnight at some magic age independent. In fact, waking up one day and discovering she can be independent may be quite threatening. One has to ease into new roles. Thus, in our opinion it is best to begin as early as possible with some decision-making so that by the time a youngster is ready to leave home, he or she will be able to make some intelligent choices based on reason as well as emotion.

We speak with the experience of parents who sent very confused messages to our children. On the one hand, we encouraged independent thinking and behavior and then turned right around and fostered dependence. One of the best examples of this kind of confused parental guidance was in matters of money. We paid our boys for certain chores; other money was given to them by family as presents. We expected them to save some of this money so they could help toward paying for something they very much wanted.

Our good intentions were a joke. When one son wanted a guitar, rather than have him empty his bank account we just bought the guitar. We thought we were being generous parents. We continued to make the same error with a lot of other items. We ended up by saying, "Oh forget it and you save for something else."

However, when they did take their money and blow it on something we thought was totally wasteful, we were annoyed. Our whole style was very confusing. We wanted to teach them some independence and began quite nobly, but then we turned right around and sent a mixed message by fostering dependence on our finances.

Learning from our own experiences, we urge parents to be as consistent as possible with their teenagers. This doesn't mean being overly demanding or hard-nosed in fostering independence. But we believe parents can do a disservice to their teenagers if they are always ready to jump in and pick up the broken pieces, if they don't encourage independence.

Learning to be independent is a critical part of your teenager's acquiring a sense of responsibility for his or her own behavior. When you are independent, when you make decisions and choices of your own, you are responsible for what you do. Taking responsibility for one's behavior is an important difference between the child and the adult. As an adult, if you make a mess of what you do, it's not likely that someone else is going to step in and cover up for you. So, helping your teenagers become increasingly independent and responsible is a central issue in helping them grow into adulthood.

The secret is starting out in small ways and gradually moving up to bigger responsibilities. The goal will be to make sure that by the time your child is ready to leave home to go to college or be on his own, he will have had a chance to manage his own affairs with a lot less input from you.

The tough question:

14 | *"What do I do when there is a crisis with my teenager?"*

"I sometimes feel like I'm living on the brink of a disaster. I never know what's going to happen next. Maybe I pay too much attention to what my son sometimes says. Maybe it's all a lot of talk? Perhaps he's trying to shock me with the stories. I fantasize sometimes about packing my suitcases and leaving. I feel I've lived through my own adolescence and problems already and a second go-around is just too much. Just when you think you've done all the right things, your kid comes home and tells you something awful that happened to some kids he knows that sends you reeling.

"I never thought in a million years the police would call me about my son. He and some friends were caught acting up one night in front of a convenience store. It was the worst moment of my life. What does one do? I can tell you how I felt. I wanted to beat some sense into him. He was lucky my husband was on a business trip. That night and for the following week I must have talked myself hoarse lecturing to him."

Mother of a seventeen-year-old boy

The tough answer:

Problem-free adolescence? We wonder if this is possible. We certainly don't know any adult who can honestly say his or her adolescence was *completely* problem or trouble free. We wonder if adolescence is a special time because of the sudden awareness of self, introspective feelings, and sensitivities of the age.

In some cases, decades later, some of the traumatic events of adolescence may leave lingering hurts. One successful businessman told us that his stomach still churns with memories of having been defeated for class president, an honor that he worked for and desperately wanted. And this happened thirty years ago!

Another parent described feeling like a nervous wreck until her daughter was asked to the junior prom. Memories of herself *not* being asked had never been forgotten. Having experienced their own share of adolescent traumas, parents sometimes find it difficult to live through another round of crises in their children.

A giant first step toward coping will be for parents to recognize and accept the fact that some crises are normal and to be expected in every adolescent's life, just as they were in your lives. The problems that generate crises are usually difficult enough for the teenager to deal with, but in some instances they can be made more complicated by a parent's emotional state.

"My son flunked a French final," one mother said. "That meant he might not be promoted. I could have died. He's a top student. He was careless. Is it right for a school to penalize a kid? I mean, where is the justice? What is learning about? Why shouldn't he have a second chance?"

Irate, she went to the teacher, the principal, and her demands were such that her son was allowed to retake the test. In retrospect, she wonders if she did her son a disservice. Her emotional reactions, particularly anger, got in the way of reason. She said later, "I should have done something like break dishes or run five miles, anything but go to school for him. He should have been made to handle the situation. It was *his* problem. I could have advised him but not made him dependent. He couldn't possibly have learned a lesson because I stepped in and took care of him.

"I blamed him for messing up his work in general, which wasn't true. It was just French. I told him he lacked responsibility, which also wasn't true. I said I was worried that if he continued to be careless about schoolwork, the rest of his education would be endangered. We started with French and I got carried away to everything else in life. I think the idea of his having to go to summer school when we had other plans was too much for me. Until I was needed, I should have stayed out of the picture. What happens the next time and the next? He won't be going through life with me holding his hand."

One of the dangers in a crisis is when parents overgeneralize. It would have been far better if this mother had focused on the immediate trauma of the moment and ***not brought up an imagined future***. Her son was upset and felt guilty even though he couldn't express himself. It can hardly be expected that he would show his mother gratitude for pointing out his current failures as well as making dire predictions about his future. When an adolescent messes up, he/she knows it. They don't need parents reminding them of the mess they are in, the errors they committed, or the impropriety of their behavior.

When a crisis occurs, your job as a parent is to provide immediate, unconditional support and, for the time being at least, to forget about trying to reform or remodel your adolescent. Your child needs to feel totally accepted and sustained regardless of what has gone on before and without any conditions attached. "If you promise to be good," or "If you change," or "If you'll listen to me in the future" are "ifs" that weaken the effectiveness of your response.

It certainly isn't easy for a parent to keep from expressing his feelings, as Eleanor's father discovered the evening he picked her up after she had left home in a tantrum and crashed the family car.

"Everything went through my mind from rage to relief that she wasn't hurt. I made arrangements for the car to be towed. I bought her coffee. I tell you I was biting my lips to make me not say what I really wanted to say. On the way home we talked about everything else but the accident. I knew she was waiting for me to explode. I let her go upstairs to sleep. In fact, the next day I didn't say anything. It was like a cat-and-mouse game.

"I finally felt myself calm down and then I brought up the accident. We talked about her responsibility to pay for the car's repair and how I felt about her running away."

We spoke to Eleanor about a month after the accident. She said that what her father did was great. She couldn't get over his not screaming at her, "maybe even hitting or something" is how she phrased it. "I was wrong," she admitted, "but his just staying so cool that night meant a lot to me."

She said that she had a couple of friends whose parents were "terrible when they had problems. They told one of my friends to leave. They said they didn't care what happened to her. She was pregnant and went to her mom who talked to her dad. She got so hysterical she had a miscarriage, which everyone felt was so lucky. No one wanted the baby. She's back home now. The whole family seems to have such a grudge against each other. I even asked my dad if it had been something like that, would he have acted the same way as he did about the car. He told me that I was his daughter and at the moment what I would probably need was a strong shoulder to cry upon, not a lecture. He was so right."

Undivided attention at the right time can have enormously important psychological effects. A crisis is a time for a parent to drop everything else if possible and be a sympathetic listener with empathic understanding and a nonjudgmental attitude.

This is clearly illustrated by an incident reported to us by the father of a teenage son who got into trouble at school. When the principal called to report that Alan was going to be expelled from school because of vandalism, Alan's father immediately dropped whatever he was doing and went to the school. This was a critical turning point in their relationship.

"My son said that he didn't think I would go to school. He was right. My first thought was to let him sweat it out. But I heard a crack in the kid's voice and I decided to drop everything and go to him. I didn't know it at the time but he wasn't involved. It was a mistake. But for Alan, my going to his side when I didn't even know the facts meant a lot to him. 'You didn't even know, Dad, it wasn't me but some other kids and still you came.' He's never forgotten what I did. There are odd times when he'll bring it up to me."

In a crisis, give your adolescent undivided attention. Don't overreact; stay focused on the problem; don't generalize to other situations and the youngster's life before or after the crisis; give all the psychological support you can; empathize and hold back on your anger. Don't moralize at the moment.

However, *after* all has calmed down, and the crisis has passed, there is a time to sit down together to find out what went wrong and what can be done in the future. With both of you somewhat toned down and relaxed, you can reach each other and effect changes in behavior. That's the time to express your feelings, talk about values, morality, and your expectation. No one can prescribe what you should do or say. However, what's going to make the difference is your having let the crisis subside a bit before you do what you feel is right for your child and for your family.

The tough question:

15 | *"Sometimes there's a conflict between fitting in with friends and being true to yourself. How can I help my teenager deal with this problem?"*

"My daughter is out of step with the other kids. It bothers me. She doesn't seem to have friends. I see other girls walking together. Friends tell me their daughters spend hours on the telephone with girlfriends—not my daughter. I think it's sad for her to be alone so much. I do what I can. I tell her to call up other girls, make plans, and do something. I honestly can't understand her. When I was her age I had tons of girlfriends."

Mother of a fifteen-year-old girl

"All the boys play baseball; my son goes to some crazy martial arts class. He says he likes karate. I told him that every kid plays baseball. Not him. It was the same when he was a little kid. Boys his age would go left, and he went right. Is he always going to be out of step with kids his age? I worry about him not fitting in, not hanging out with other kids. My wife says it's a no-win situation. If he did hang out with other kids on Saturday nights, he could run into trouble. Better that, as far as I am concerned, than always doing his own thing. I have this feeling he's programmed differently from other kids."

Father of a fifteen-year-old boy

The tough answer:

There are many myths about adolescents that are part of the popular culture. One pervasive myth is that American teenagers are a closely knit group of kids who behave, dress, and even speak like each other. If we were to believe many observers of the American scene, we would assume all American teenagers are pretty much the same.

While it is true that adolescents do share some common developmental characteristics and there are similarities among teenagers with respect to age-related behaviors, in no shape or form can we discount the many individual differences. Certainly, there are teenagers who run around in groups, hang out together, and engage in hours of telephone conversations. But there are plenty of others who do not conform to this stereotype. They walk alone, "dancing to the tune in their own heads."

We happen to be very sensitive to this question raised by any number of parents who were concerned when they had kids that they felt were "different" because they were not part of the larger adolescent group culture. As adolescents we vacillated on both sides of the fence. On the one hand, we were loners, and on the other hand, we were immersed in group activities.

Lois had grown up with a father who spouted all sorts of aphorisms such as: "do your own thing, follow your own direction and not the group's. He who walks alone walks the furthest. Be the master of yourself. Don't bend like a willow to a group's demands. What would you do if everyone jumped off a cliff; would you jump too?" In contrast, her mother was a popular member and president of every group she joined, and she was involved with dozens of organizations.

Joel shared the same contrasting parents: a father who simply did his own thing with a total indifference to the group and a mother who relished every phone call and club presidency. Thus, we straddled a fence and sent mixed messages to our own kids. Don't bother with the group. Be sure you have friends. Do your own thing no matter what. Be part of the larger society.

We thought we were unique in our feelings as teenagers, being a curious mixture of outgoingness and withdrawal, but in adulthood we have discovered a vast number of other people who shared this same dichotomy. Thus, what we thought was so unique about us turns out to be quite common!

This conflict about inner and other directedness is one of the central psychological issues of our culture and it is during adolescence that each of us experiences this conflict in an equally compelling form. There is probably no other stage of life when the need for peer support, the need to belong to a group outside of the family is stronger. Teenagers are breaking ties with their parents, trying out new roles, facing new demands from the environment, and experiencing dramatic changes physically as well as psychologically.

Therefore, the need for some reassurance from others, the need for social acceptance and social approval, is greater than ever before. Parental acceptance and approval at this stage are not enough. Teenagers need the acceptance, reassurance, and approval of peers. Thus, it is important for parents not to fight the teenager's need to be accepted and to be approved of by peers. An adolescent's desire to be part of a group is a normal part of growing up.

On the other hand, there is a price paid for peer support and peer conformity. To be accepted by a group demands some degree of conformity to group norms, using the same kind of language, dressing in similar styles, sharing the same tastes and values. For example, the style of clothing may be so similar that an observer from another country might assume American teenagers are wearing uniforms.

However, while it is true that adolescents may have a compelling need to conform to a group and to receive the psychological support of the group that encourages them to conform to the group's norms, an even more profound psychological problem arises from the tension or need to gain a sense of individuality.

This means **breaking away** from the group if need be, following one's own "inner voice," interests, and values that may be incongruent with those of the group. When children are young, parents sometimes slip into the habit of keeping score. "My son has been invited to a birthday party every Saturday since the beginning of the year." "My daughter had kids calling her constantly for play dates."

These are comments some parents say with pride. Popularity with other kids is a highly valuable attribute in our culture. Teachers may even rate children according to their acceptance or status within the class. However, not every child is going to be the first selected. Not every youngster is going to win a popularity contest or even be in the running.

The greatest service a parent can do is to **step back** when a child reaches adolescence and let the teenager develop relationships and interact with others at his or her own pace. This may mean having friends or sometimes being alone. Rather than push your child to make friends, do whatever you can to involve your youngster in activities where he or she meets other teenagers with similar interests.

One mother told us our advice was fine and good but did we have any idea of what it was like for her and her husband to see their sixteen-year-old daughter sitting at home on weekend nights, knowing that other kids were out having a great time? She felt she had to "push" her daughter a little bit for her own good.

In this instance our suggestion was that their eagerness to do something would only create further problems. There was nothing they should do and nothing they could do except be interested and supportive of any of their daughter's interests, which in this case happened to be music. Any suggestion or hint of pushing her to go out and develop friendships or make plans that may not materialize could only be hurtful.

Yes, their daughter was out of step with her classmates. She was "dancing to a different tune." Their responsibility was to pay attention to their teenager's inner directed interests by encouraging her to explore her own values. Respect for their daughter's individuality was most important. Finding music groups that she could join could be helpful.

But what was going to be most important would be encouraging their daughter to be herself. She didn't need the added burden of parental worries and concerns. "Don't you have any friends you can call? Why doesn't anyone call you?" When parental pressure ceased, given time, this young teenager did find others who shared her musical interests.

"I never thought it would happen," said her mother, "but in her senior year she had a group of boys and girls who all played in the school orchestra come to the house. It was her idea to plan this party. I don't know who was more thrilled— she or I."

It's not always easy for some parents to stay in the background. Perhaps these parents identify far too much, remembering their own lonely teen years, awkwardness, self-doubts or concerns, and, therefore, wanting to do everything they can to make sure their kids don't go through what they did while growing up.

Whatever the motivation, it probably is a wise idea for both parents to recognize the need for their adolescent to be part of a group but also to appreciate and respect the adolescent's right to be different.

Adolescents must have a chance to discover their own internal directions, to become aware of their inner-directed impulses and to trust their own values. Each of us has to learn to make choices and judgments independent of others and to develop our own potential as a unique individual.

When your adolescent is in conflict between conforming to a group and fulfilling his or her own individuality, don't try to minimize the stress he or she might feel about being different from friends. Do what you can to encourage your teenager to become a genuinely inner-directed person.

The direction your teenager takes may be quite different from your dreams and aspirations. Your role is not to live your teenager's life for him or her. Rather, do what you can to encourage your child to explore and discover his or her own values.

The tough question:

16 | *"What should I do if my teenager seems to lack self-esteem?"*

"Everybody makes fun of me, even the way I look," my daughter told me. "When she said that, it broke my heart. She thinks she's ugly. She isn't. She's at an awkward stage. I tried to explain this to her. How many times, I told her, has she herself told me about some movie star who thought she was unattractive as a teenager.

"It doesn't seem to help. She stands in the bathroom staring at the mirror. She won't listen. All she keeps telling me is that she isn't pretty. I have to listen to her reciting names of girls at school who are pretty. The boys, everyone, say they're pretty.

"I've done everything I can think of to try and get her to stop making fun of herself. I told her that she's beautiful in my eyes. That was a terrible mistake. She got very angry and told me my saying that meant she wasn't pretty. Of course, I would say something like that because I was her mother. She told me never, never to say that again. It was an insult. She's a very good student. She has so many wonderful qualities. This constant business of being beautiful is making all of us depressed."

Mother of a sixteen-year-old girl

"My son lost his self-confidence. I think it happened after he got into high school. He was a star in Little League. Then when he started high school he ran into a lot of bigger guys who played ball a lot better than he could. That started the downward cycle. He didn't make the team.

"First, it was baseball. Then his schoolwork started to slip. He's got a couple of buddies he hangs out with, but I see signs of him withdrawing into himself. His face broke out in pimples. I think the way he felt had something to do with it. Then he started wearing his hair long to cover up his face, so naturally we tried talking to him about the way he looked. I try not to bug him. But how can I sit back and not offer help? Isn't that what a parent is supposed to do? He's my son. I love him very much."

Mother of a seventeen-year-old boy

The tough answer:

Am I pretty? Am I handsome? Am I macho? Do I have a nice figure? Am I good at sports? Am I smart? Am I good at anything? All of us can think back to when we were teenagers, remembering periods of self-doubt, concerns about our abilities, appearance, and feelings of unpopularity.

Not too long ago we were involved in a large-scale evaluation study of young college students. How vividly we recall interviews with high school beauty queens, class valedictorians, class presidents, and top-ranked high school athletes. Repeatedly, we listened to stories of how, during high school, they often felt unattractive and inadequate. The entire research team had the same reaction. The feelings these youngsters had seemed to be impossible to believe given their appearance and achievements.

Teenagers frequently mistakenly assume they are alone with their thoughts of inadequacy. They are very certain that every one of their classmates is self-assured, confident, beautiful or handsome, poised, and smart. They are an exception. "Poor me. I'm at the bottom of the heap." Of course, these feelings change from time to time. It's just not easy for a teenager to accept the fact that lack of self-esteem, confidence, and sureness about who one is and what one looks like is a very common feeling.

I (Lois) attended a *fiftieth* high school reunion. Classmates I hadn't seen since graduation attended. Each of us had a chance to get up and make a few comments about ourselves then and now. We were all stunned to discover how ugly the prettiest girl in the class had felt about herself and how inadequate and dumb the smartest boy had thought he was.

Although telling your youngest that *all* teenagers have periods of self-doubt might not make them feel better, it is an important step for you to **understand** and **empathize** with the feelings your youngster is expressing. When a teenage girl asks if she's pretty, nothing wounds her more than a concerned mother saying, "You are beautiful in *my* eyes." That's the last thing she wants to hear. She wants to be beautiful in the *world's* eyes.

Rather than come up with some fancy, generalized answer, it might be more helpful to talk about her specific features, for example, the color of her eyes, the shape of her face, hair, specific abilities, or talents.

Not feeling good about yourself is a perfectly reasonable adolescent reaction. It takes a little work to shift their attitudes from the negative to the positive. However, as we know, every teenager has a reservoir of strengths and this is a time for parents to focus on them.

Katy's mother used this approach one afternoon when her daughter asked about her singing voice. Desperately wanting to be a member of the choir, she asked her mother for an evaluation of her voice. She stood up and sang. Katy's mother was painfully aware that her daughter was tone deaf.

However, rather than take Katy down a peg or two, with an objective evaluation, she compared her daughter's singing voice with her other skills. Her suggestion was that Katy might focus on her natural gifts rather than try to be a choir member. "After all," her mother said, "there are girls in the choir who could never match your artistic talent."

Helping a teenager to go with his or her strengths is all important. The too-small boy who wants to be a basketball player or the teenage girl who aspires to be a dancer and lacks fluidity of movement is not uncommon. Teenagers have fantasies, as we all do, and they see themselves playing roles for which they are not suited. In my dreams I (Lois) glided over ice, twirling and jumping. In early adolescence I reluctantly gave up this dream when I finally faced the fact that I couldn't even skate well backward.

It isn't necessary for a parent to dash cold water on all dreams, but it is helpful if a parent does some active guidance in helping teenagers identify their real skills, special talents, unique abilities. All too often teenagers, whatever the motivation, may try to accomplish or move in a direction for which they are not suited. When this happens, loss of self-esteem and confidence is inevitable.

Kevin, a young teenager, wanted desperately to be a scientist. He had all sorts of grandiose dreams of working in a laboratory and making great discoveries. While it is true that his science grades were acceptable, he was not a shining star and over the months of his junior year, time after time his ego was deflated by low grades.

"I'm no good at anything," was his angry outburst. The fact was, in terms of his scientific skills, he wasn't all that great; however, when it came to his social and organizational skills, such as serving as manager for the school's basketball team, he was outstanding. "Anyone can be a manager," he protested.

The fact is that just "anyone" couldn't be a manager, and it was important for his parents to help Kevin realize this fact. Kevin had a special talent for organization. He did not have a distinctive gift for laboratory science.

Being successful in life depends on choosing the right situation. If we're in the wrong situation, we're uncomfortable, we feel inferior, and we're much less likely to realize our potential. However, in the right situation, each of us can shine. Parents can help teenagers find the right situation, the place where their talents are appreciated.

There are right and wrong situations for every person. Obviously, kids won't always have a choice. School doesn't permit such freedom. In general, conformity is demanded. There aren't always enough choices in the curriculum to accommodate great differences. Youngsters are assigned to teachers whose personalities may be totally at variance with a given student.

Your child may be placed in a classroom that is all wrong, and there won't be much you can do to alter the situation. The rationale is that everything can't be perfect, and the teenage years are a good time to learn to adapt. This situation can mean difficulties and bumpy times not only for the child, but also for the parents who have to live through these rough periods.

However, there are some things parents can do to make everyone's life more enjoyable when this happens. Encourage your child to look elsewhere for opportunities to excel. Seek out situations where your youngster can be appreciated and have his or her skills recognized, circumstances where your child's abilities are recognized and appreciated. School represents only *one* part of a student's life.

One teenager we spoke with reported how she had been overlooked for parts in school musicals. "I had the best voice. Everyone told me this was so. The music director didn't like me. When I didn't even get a tiny part, I was devastated. I never wanted to sing again." Her self-esteem was gone. The desire for music lessons ceased.

A resourceful mother searched out a local theatrical company in the community. Rather than focus on the negatives, she encouraged her daughter to become involved in the local group where she was soon given leading roles. In fact, the outside situation was more appropriate for her talents than the school productions.

In the course of growing up, everyone meets both success and failure. No one is entirely successful in everything he or she tries to do. Each of us has particular talents and skills that best fit certain situations and don't fit so well in others. So, success and failure depend not only on an individual's talents and skills, but also on how well the individual's style and abilities fit the demands of a given situation.

It is only normal for young people to attribute success or failure entirely to the individual or entirely to the situation. It is therefore most important that they learn to see the world in terms of the interaction between the individual and the situation. More specifically, teenagers must gain some awareness of the situations in which their own interests, talents, abilities, and personal styles fit best, and those in which they don't fit so well.

Gaining this awareness is not always an easy process. It demands a self-examination of one's own trials and errors, identifying the situations in which one has succeeded and those in which one has failed, and this process can be emotionally stressful. It requires some objectivity in reflecting on one's own past performances.

The tough question:

17 | *"What do I do about limits, privileges, and responsibilities?"*

"My son says he's old enough to make his own decisions. Well, that's just great. What he forgets is that he's living at home, in our house. We pay the bills. He can't just do whatever he wants. There are obligations to the rest of the family. It's so hard to get him to understand this simple fact. You'd think I was asking for the moon when all I'll say is, 'Clean up your room.'

"The other day I told him that my having to do the laundry— his laundry, no less—is not the worst thing that could happen in my life. I have a responsibility to him. The family has responsibilities to each other. We can't live pretending the family doesn't exist.

Mother of a seventeen-year-old boy

The tough answer:

Kids wanting it all: privileges without responsibilities, freedom without any limitations on behavior. Does all of this sound familiar? The tug-of-war that so often occurs regarding limits, privileges, and responsibilities often becomes an issue between parents and their adolescent sons and daughters. Little children love to help parents. Adolescents may assume a sour expression when asked to perform a minimal chore.

Even though teenagers can feel imposed upon when asked to help at home, these same kids cam sometimes be relentless in pushing their parents for more and more privileges. "I feel like I'm always bargaining with my son," one mother commented. "Everything is a trade-off. When he wants something, he doesn't give up. Right now he's after me about using my car whenever he wants to."

For many teenagers, the first big demand for more privileges with or without bargaining often revolves around using the family automobile. Many cultures have ceremonies to mark a child's entrance into the adult world. For an American youngster, a driver's license signals adulthood. However, as parents well know, passing a driver's test, getting a license, having unrestricted use of a family car, and being an adult may be very separate issues.

From the first day our son obtained his driver's license, we were concerned; perhaps scared is a better term. Thus, in the first few months after he had his license we managed to come up with a variety of excuses why he couldn't drive alone.

Suddenly we had pressing engagements. The car's battery needed recharging; we wanted to have the tire treads checked because we were concerned that the car needed new tires. If he would only wait a little longer, we assured him, he would be able to drive alone.

The "little while" stretched into weeks. His patience was wearing thin. Our trying to fend off his using the car was hardly conducive to a happy relationship. Backed against the wall, we finally had no choice but to give in to his request.

Every parent can share our tension that fateful evening when we sat in the living room, listening to the car's motor being turned on. We sneaked looks out the window to watch the vehicle ease down the driveway, holding our breaths as he turned the car into the street. Before handing him the keys, he had been given a final barrage of warnings about speed, safety, and any of a dozen other precautions. In his excitement to get out of the house as quickly as possible, we were certain he hadn't paid attention to any of our last-minute instructions.

Waiting for his return after that initial solo trip was agony. When the telephone rang, we jumped. The torture intensified as the hours passed. Sleep was impossible. Sitting in the kitchen at midnight drinking endless cups of coffee, we imagined the worst. Finally, at about dawn, unable to hold out any longer, we notified the police, giving a full description of the car and driver. Our only relief was when the police told us that no accidents had been reported.

As we stood in front of the garage waiting for the town police who said they would be over to take a report, the car magically appeared, moving slowly down the street. There was our son unharmed, gripping the wheel, sitting in that stiff, upright position characteristic of new drivers.

"Where the hell have you been?"

During the long hours of waiting, we had been sentimental. If only we could see him and he was safe, we would be eternally appreciative. Thank you, dear God, for answering our prayers. When he did appear, obviously safe, sentiment fled, and we lashed out in fury.

"Give us the damn keys to the car. This is the last time you ever take the car. Where is your sense of responsibility? How dare you make us suffer like this? We were up all night."

The local police arrived, heard our angry voices, listened for a few minutes before smiling, and drove away.

Doors inside the house slammed. A distraught mother cried.

Our son finally managed to break into a tirade, "Won't you listen to my side of the story?"

"There is no side to your story. You were wrong. OK, go ahead and come up with some creative excuse."

"I was all right."

"How could we know that?"

We dared not tell him our fantasies. Our imaginations had run wild. We were definitely out of control. When we finally shut up for a moment, he was able to tell us exactly what had occurred. He had gone to a party. At 2 A.M., he fully expected to return home. However, he said that he had had a beer and became very sleepy. Our warnings about having anything to drink and driving had been effective. He returned to the house where the party was held and with a group of his friends he camped out on the family room floor.

He had been shocked to wake up at 6 A.M. It had crossed his mind that we might be worried, but he figured we were asleep and wouldn't know he wasn't in his bed. Not wanting to wake us, he just returned home. Since he was fine, he couldn't imagine why we were upset. Why hadn't we gone to sleep? Our panic, fears, near-hysteria at his not returning the entire night were incomprehensible to him.

When we finally regained some rationality, we realized the mistake was ours. Although we had bombarded him with all sorts of driving advice, we had neglected to say anything about curfews or checking in with us. A lot of anxiety could have been avoided if we had made explicit ground rules. We explained that our feelings of concern, justified or not, had been real.

In the future, it was only fair that, in return for using the car, he would have certain limits and responsibilities. We had to know where he was going and the approximate time of his return. If for any reason there were unexpected delays, he was to telephone. The lateness of the hour did not matter.

The following Saturday evening he again asked to use the car. "Don't worry," he assured us with what we later realized was a sly smile, "I got your message."

We settled down to watch a movie. Starting at 8 P.M. calls came in every twenty minutes. After the sixth call, when our watching was interrupted, we relented and called a halt to the checking in.

It's not easy for adolescents on their way to independence to realize the depth of parental concern. They are much too wrapped up in themselves to really stop and take another's perspective, particularly if that other person is a parent. More often than not adolescence is a time of *self-worry, self-concern, and self-interest.* Adolescents may even bask in their own feelings of "nobody loves me; nobody cares about me; I don't count for much."

Elena, a seventeen-year-old, told us how jarred she felt when she realized how much her mother cared. "She did it in a funny way. I came home real late one night from a party. She had no idea where I was. When I came home she was waiting for me, and she started at me something awful, and then she slapped me. I was stunned. She never had hit me before.

"Then she started crying, and I ended up comforting her instead of the other way around. She told me she was so worried because I hadn't come home at a reasonable hour. Her head was pounding and she had knots in her stomach.

"She told me it was worry, anger, relief, which seems weird to me. But I guess I saw how much she cared. You know, I was kind of surprised. I had no idea. Anyhow, I promised her that I would let her know where I was going, and if I was going to be late, to let her know. She told me she wants me to have freedom and she won't be checking constantly, but she has to know I'm OK."

Family tensions can be eased when you work out your teenager's privileges, limits, and responsibilities **together** rather than imposing your expectations. It's far better to do this *before* the fact rather than *after.* One parent told us her son had volunteered their house for a party. "He told me none of the other parents would let the party be held and, besides, we have a pretty big basement. I was annoyed, but my son was quite insistent and I thought why not? This way I will know what's going on. But I set down some rules and told my son that he and his friends could work them out in their own way. I didn't want smoking, drinking, and I didn't want outsiders crashing the party.

"They, in turn, asked that my husband and I not be home. I said, 'OK, we'll go out for some of the evening, and, when we come home, we won't go downstairs.' But I told them point blank; if things got out of hand we would intervene.

"We did all this in a very matter-of-fact way. I was surprised. The party was a big success. I think having the kids know beforehand what the rules were made a big difference."

Establishing and maintaining limits with adolescents isn't all that easy. How does one stay consistent? More than that, sometimes parents, including ourselves, aren't sure which limits are reasonable and which are unusually severe. It's easy, too, to mistake being overindulgent and permissive with love. We want to make sure that our teenagers know we love them, so we give in to a lot of whims and desires we feel aren't all that great or maybe even make us uncomfortable.

One concern some parents expressed was a fear of defying their adolescent. "I've read enough horror stories," one parent told us, "about kids whose parents were strict or had a lot of rules and what happens in those families." We certainly shared this worry. When our sons were teenagers, it was the height of the cult era. Several teenagers we knew personally had walked out on their families simply because their parents had imposed what we thought were reasonable rules. Although we had no idea, nor does anyone, what goes on behind closed doors in other people's homes, when we do hear stories that are disturbing it's only natural that we feel some tremors and think, "There but for the grace of God go I."

Anything can be carried to an extreme. However, from a developmental point of view, the issue of limits is especially significant during adolescence. The teenager is living through a time of tremendous growth and development with enormous physical changes as well as changes in personal and social expectations. Psychological instability, wavering, restlessness, and hesitation are not uncommon. Having limits of some sort can serve as a developmental bridge from childhood into adulthood. It's actually comforting for the teenager to have a stable, well-structured external world. Thus, limits and responsibilities are comforting not only for the parent but also for the teenager.

The parental task of establishing limits for children changes as the child grows older. When children are very young, simple directives impose limits; "Play near the house. Eat your dinner. Do your homework. Go to bed." Few parents and few small children really sit down and have long, involved discussions about the rationale behind expected behaviors.

By the time our children are adolescents, simple directives may not be very effective. It comes as a bit of shock when we discover adolescents in our house who don't bend easily to our demands, who won't conform to our wishes, who don't jump when a command is given.

We think it's cute when a four-year-old, in response to an order to go to bed, asks, "Why?" We even encourage a lot of questioning.

When a teenager questions, we aren't all that eager to engage in long discussions or explanations. "Why can't I stay up as long as I want to? Why can't I have sex? Why can't I smoke pot?"

The relatively simple questions of childhood suddenly become complex and can't be dismissed with simple, short cut answers. In many cases, we may not even have answers and our own lack of certainty makes us uncomfortable in being put on the spot. More often than not, we react with irritation and annoyance.

"Why do I have to explain?" argues one father. "I pay the bills. I support my son. As long as he lives at home, he damn well better listen."

It's not easy for this father to give up his authoritarian power. It's not easy to switch to a democratic relationship when the issues involved are more than simple challenges about extra desserts or how much television can be watched. "My daughter better not sleep around," said one mother. "I don't want her to have sex. She knows how we feel." "Does she really?" we asked. More than a simple "no" is required on your part; explanations are necessary. Does she know the **reasons** for your feelings? Have you discussed *why* you believe sex at fifteen, in fact sex outside of marriage, is morally wrong?

Although discussions between parents and their teenagers about issues of sexual behavior may involve a good deal of tension, in most families the most frequent conflicts concern other aspects of life.

In one of our studies we asked teenagers what areas or topics caused the most conflict between them and their parents. The main areas for dissension were: curfews, school performance, money, choice of friends, and personal habits (appearance, clothes, etc). However, regardless of the specific area of conflict, from the teenager's point of view the most important issue was the way parents go about the process of establishing limits. In the same study we mentioned earlier, we asked adolescents what they wished for most in relation to their parents. The most frequent response was a desire for parental respect for their opinions, reflected by their parents talking *with* them rather than *at* them.

This finding provides a crucial key to dealing with the problem of establishing limits. By the time your child reaches adolescence, it's no longer a matter of issuing simple commands and directives. You have to talk *with* your teenagers, not *at* them, clearly expressing your own feelings, thoughts, and values, but also listening to and really hearing their views. In other words, establishing limits is achieved most effectively when parents and their teenagers go about the process with mutual respect and a genuine effort to understand each other's point of view.

Some parents might see this process as unduly demanding, and it certainly does require more time and effort than simply issuing an order. But in the long run, taking some time and effort to work out reasonable limits with your teenager is likely to save you a lot of headaches and needless arguments. From time to time, review your expectations to keep them in line with the teenager's increasing maturity. Deciding upon fair and reasonable limits and responsibilities together doesn't mean that all problems in a given area will be resolved for the remainder of adolescence. You're going to have to expect your teenager to *test* the limits. This makes sense. You certainly can't expect an almost eighteen-year-old to live within the same set of limits as a fourteen-year-old. Thus, no matter how fair limits, privileges, and responsibilities may seem at one age, they may be totally inappropriate a few years later.

As an adolescent grows older, responsibilities and privileges should increase appropriately. Remember that responsibility stimulates psychological growth, but *too much* responsibility too soon in a person's life can be stifling, frustrating, and make the teenager feel overburdened. Parents who have placed a great deal of responsibility on their teenagers often are impressed with the maturity and capabilities their teenagers demonstrate. While from the outside the performance may be impressive, the teenager may come away with another perspective.

My (Lois's) parents owned a summer camp for children. As a teenager, I was expected to undertake counselor responsibilities far beyond my years, for example, managing programs and being an instructor in many activities. While other teenagers played, I was the mature, responsible sixteen-year-old. I confess to a great deal of resentment, not so much then but later in life, when I felt I had missed out on some carefree teenage experiences.

Other adults who for one reason or another had to undertake similar adultlike responsibilities during their adolescence shared my later feelings. "Other kids played," one woman said. "I ran the family store after school. I had to earn all the money."

If a family's circumstances necessitate that teenagers assume adult roles, there may not be a choice for parents other than to depend on their children. However, if it isn't an absolute financial necessity, we think it best to keep the responsibilities you impose in *reasonable proportion*, never forgetting that too much too soon may make your child feel overburdened and frustrated.

On the other hand, there is an equal danger of giving an adolescent too many privileges, the consequence of which is an unrealistic view of life. An overindulged adolescent is ill-prepared to face the normal demands of young adulthood. Therefore, privileges, responsibilities, and limits must be kept in harmony with each other, each increasing as the adolescent moves toward adult status.

One last word before you involve your adolescent in the decision-making process. Make sure that you have clarified your own views about limits, privileges, and responsibilities. Try to be reasonable and understanding. Then and only then sit down with your teenager to work out a balance between your wishes and what your teenager sees as fair. If you're called "unfair, unreasonable, dictatorial," remember to keep your cool. Chances are that your teenager feels defensive and/or threatened. Try to understand the reasons for these feelings. Attack and counterattack won't help you achieve your goal: a safe, productive life for your teenager.

The tough question:

18

"How can I best help my teenager learn how to handle money?"

Our grandsons have had bank accounts from first grade on. If they're saving for something special, they've requested money instead of presents. They know certain expensive purchases require their contribution.

Are we impressing you with this fact? Perhaps not. Well, let us assure you that the first time we discovered all this was happening, we listened with wide-eyed astonishment. Could this grandson actually be the son of the father *we had raised*, who one year emptied a bank account because he decided he wanted to buy skis that were used exactly once?

One joy of grandparenting is observing how many mistakes that you made in child-rearing are being corrected in the next generation. Of course, the parents will make their own mistakes, but in our family one mistake neither of our sons will make is not teaching their own children about the value of money.

In our studies of parents, we have consistently found that many parents are concerned about teaching their children the value of money. "Educational expenses today cost fortunes; my day-to-day expenses are enormous. I can't let my kid assume that money grows on trees," one father commented.

The tough answer:

We have lots of advice about money, advice we certainly didn't follow. How a family thinks about money depends on their own expenses. We were children of the Great Depression so, of course, money concerns and worries loomed over the family. Thus, we now realize that we bent over backward in an effort to make sure our children wouldn't grow up with nagging worries about money matters. Parents often behave this way. If something bothered them in their childhood they will make an effort to do exactly the opposite with their children.

This was a mistake. Because of our personal concerns, there was a gap in our sons' understanding of money, its relationship to work, earning, and other concepts that are important for everyone to know. Our sons didn't have allowances; they were given money for their needs. Working outside the home was not encouraged, perhaps even frowned upon, in our belief that they should put all their energies into schoolwork.

One son recently asked us, "Why didn't you let me have a job while I was in high school?" He felt that kind of experience would have been useful preparation for adulthood. He pays his son for work in the yard and has encouraged us to hire our grandson for various chores.

We tried to explain our position: "Going to school was your job." Our reasoning was that we had jobs to earn money. Our son's job was his schoolwork. Unfortunately, this is unrealistic.

Everyone goes to school, and school is not a job. Several years ago we were involved in an international study concerned with teenagers and part-time work. Results indicated that American teenagers frequently held part-time jobs during the school year, averaging more than twenty hours per week.

Some educators believe that part-time work interferes with schoolwork and curtails opportunities to participate in valuable extracurricular activities. Interestingly enough, these negative opinions about part-time work were *not* shared by students, many of whom felt that part-time work increased their appreciation of money, taught them values, improved their relationships with other people ("I have to learn to get along," noted one girl), and, in general, gave students a sense of responsibility and independence.

Whether or not you encourage your teenager to have a part-time job is of course an individual matter. Much depends on such factors as family resources and teenagers' material needs and their desires. Obviously, a part-time job which erodes into school or study time should be discouraged. However, we believe that some part-time work can provide opportunities to learn about the world outside of school, as well as develop realistic attitudes and values regarding money. There is no general solution to this issue that fits everyone, but parents should take an active role in helping their teenager achieve a balance of activities appropriate for each individual.

The tough question:

19 | *"What if I think my teenager's friends are a bad influence?"*

"I can't stand some of my child's friends. Recently, my son started hanging out with kids I wish he never had met. The other day I came home from work. There were four so-called friends in the kitchen. My stomach churned. One was smoking. The others would not look me in the face. I wish you could have seen what they were wearing. They looked like gutter kids. Each of them needed a haircut and probably a shower. My first thought was that these kids are 'bad news.' At my insistence they left. My son got angry, yelling at me, 'You don't like my friends.'

"'You're so right,' I told him. 'Where did you pick those kids up?' My tone clearly meant I thought they were garbage.

"'They go to my school. They're my friends.'

"'I suggest you take a second look at them and find others. You might just as well know how I feel. I don't ever want to see those kids in this house again.'

"He stormed out of the room. The next day he wouldn't speak to me. We're still having problems. He's accused me of never liking any of his friends. That's simply not the case."

Mrs. R., mother of a sixteen-year-old boy

The tough answer:

We have a hunch, Mrs. R., that on the evening after the confrontation with your son, you felt pretty nostalgic. You thought about his childhood, a time when you had absolute control over who came to your house. Perhaps there was a child who overturned the goldfish bowl on the living room rug and laughed at your reprimands. You told your son that was the end of that child ever having another play date at your home. Your son obeyed. He didn't have a choice.

It's very upsetting when we discover that our children manage to find friends in the most unlikely places, kids we simply don't like. Anger or fear may be involved because we're scared that "bad" friends will negatively influence our children.

However, before we move into the tough answer, we want to make sure, Mrs. R., that you aren't jumping to the wrong conclusion based on a few superficial clues. We'd like to share an experience from our life when we made that kind of mistake.

Many years ago when one son was in high school the appearance of a young woman he dated stunned us. We immediately thought the worst. Her unruly, long, unkempt hair was barely tolerable; the all-too-revealing clothes unacceptable. Garish jewelry, elongated, false, painted nails added more negatives to the overall picture. In that era any girl who had this kind of image was considered to have loose morals. We were afraid she would lead our son into perdition.

A recent event presents a great twist to this story. I (Lios) had a medical appointment. My regular physician was absent. A charming, young woman doctor entered the room, hugged me, and said, "I'm covering for Doctor X. How wonderful to see you again after all these years. I can't wait to hear what's happened to everyone."

Aware of my confusion, she asked, "Have I changed that much? With the kind of hours I put in, no wonder my hair is turning gray!"

We reminisced about the past when she had dated our son.

It would be nice, we suppose, if some of your teenager's friends or your own teenager could skip the stage when it seems as if they are wearing some outlandish Halloween costume with a strange sort of mask. We certainly felt that way. But the example we cited demonstrates that, in some cases, external appearances may be a total contradiction of the youngster's real nature and values.

Snap judgments we made about that young woman just because of her style were really unfair. The reality is, on occasion, many otherwise intelligent, wonderful teenagers are going to "act out." The easiest way to "act out" is through extreme clothes, hairstyles, makeup, or jewelry.

On the other hand, we definitely are in complete agreement with Mrs. R. and other worried parents about the importance of being aware and sensitive when it comes to your youngsters' friends. It's been well documented that peers have an enormous impact on teenage behavior. Some professionals have gone to an extreme, saying that peer groups are *everything,* and parental opinions or influence don't carry much weight.

We do not agree with this viewpoint. There's no doubt in our minds that peers can and do exert a strong pull on a teenager's behavior; however, it is also a fact that parental values and guidance still have an effect on a youngster's thinking. Your teenager has lived as a family member for a long time. Your family values, beliefs, and behaviors have undoubtedly made a dramatic and lasting impression even if it's not always obvious. Sometimes family values don't show up until adulthood!

However, as we all know, the teen years are a time when youngsters begin straining at bonds that link them to their family. No matter how great a relationship you have with your kids there will be times when they challenge your values, accusing you of being hopelessly out-of-date. Friends' opinions seem far more important. A vital part of growing up involves a stage when teenagers inevitably pull away from parental authority and influence.

Does this mean parents should sit back and let external influences take over? Definitely not! However, breaking off or discouraging undesirable relationships does take *tact and diplomacy*. "I will ground my daughter first before I let her go out with one of the boys who called and asked her for a date," one father told us.

While it is true that he may ground her successfully this time, he may not be so successful the next time around. "Do tact and diplomacy mean I have to tiptoe around my kid, always guarding my thoughts, afraid to say what I think?" asked another parent.

Emphatically not! What must be changed are not your values but how you go about communicating an effective message. First of all, parents must realize the teenager is no longer that little kid who can be told that the girl who ripped out all the hair of your daughter's new doll is unwelcome as a friend. When children are small, we can hand down these kinds of dictums.

Although we can't do this with teenagers, it's still very important that parents clarify their beliefs. If you try to remain silent, chances are that you will reveal your negative opinions in any number of subtle ways. I (Lois) remember many times when I thought I was being very circumspect by not coming right out and saying what I thought about some of our sons' friends. I was caught up short when I was told in no uncertain terms that my "pursed lips" or grimaces gave my reactions away. And they went on and described their father's way of showing disapproval. "He starts clenching his fists. His shoulders get squared. He doesn't have to say anything, that's for sure."

It just makes sense, right from the start, to be up front, open, and direct about your attitudes and feelings. Adults shouldn't

forget that they have lived a lot longer and have had more experience than a teenager. There is an *obligation* to share some of
this knowledge. It took us a long time to practice this in our
own home.

When our sons were teenagers, we often bent over backward
not to say anything. As psychologists, we are very familiar with
childhood research that states domineering, controlling parents run the risk of creating problems. Researchers feel that
children must have ample opportunities to learn from their
own experiences. Because of these studies, we were always trying to be cautious not to make too many judgments, fearful of
the psychological effects on our boys.

Now we do not want to discount all these academic theories,
but, over the years, we have come to the conclusion that caution
is needed about how far parents should go in putting theory into
practice. We can overdo interference just as we can be much too
reticent about volunteering opinions or judgments. There were
far too many times we went to one extreme or another.

For example, we remember a time when one son was
involved in a very detrimental relationship with a special
friend. His feelings were hurt repeatedly. We didn't say anything. We suffered in silence, wondering when our son would
catch on to the results. Many years later we were talking about
this incident in relationship to his children. His comment was,
"Why didn't you say anything? Why did you let me stumble
blindly? It was such a waste of my time and energy."

We talked about our rationale, our concern about interfer-
ing, although we admitted to worrying privately. His comment
was we had a made a **big** mistake. According to him, the least
we could have done was to have told him what we thought so
he could have made his own decision. "With my kids, when I
see something wrong, like a bad relationship, I sure tell them.
There's nothing wrong in parents protecting their kids."

In a similar instance, another son's so-called friend was
someone we didn't trust. Sly, conniving, manipulative, this
youngster was the most popular kid in the school. Everyone

wanted to be his friend. Aware, yet not wanting to be intrusive parents, we didn't say anything. The friendship ended when this other youngster, jealous of our son's academic performance, stole a major term paper out of our son's book bag and shredded it. Our son did not have another copy and had to start over from scratch.

Should we have said anything at the time, mentioning our concerns? Of course we were wrong not to do so. We should have told him about our feelings, what we had observed, and let our son make his own decision about the relationship.

The key to parental intervention, we feel, is *how, what, and when to intervene.* Obviously, it's all wrong to intervene every time something isn't exactly right in your opinion. However, if the problem really troubles you, and you think there's danger of any sort involved, it's important for you to act.

Crucial in all this is remembering to be restrained and diplomatic. We admit that's not always easy. A recent incident with a teenage grandson, however, revealed to us the positive results if a situation is handled this way.

One of his so-called friends was a child we disliked for what we felt was good reason. First of all, we had overheard this youngster openly making fun of his parents and criticizing all grandparents, including us, as being people to avoid. You can imagine our reactions. Furthermore we didn't do a very good job, expression-wise, of hiding our feelings when we were in the presence of this teenager.

"You don't like K.," our grandson finally said one afternoon. "But he is my friend, not yours. I have my own friends just like you have yours. I don't go around telling you who should be your friends."

"Of course," we agreed. "You have your friends. Whom you decide to be friends with is your decision, not ours. However, we have a right to our opinions."

Curious, he asked, "What don't you like about K?"

"Remember," we told him, "you are your own person. We're reflecting only our opinions. K. is not our friend." And, in our very best rational tone we described how we felt about the other boy, mentioning what he said about his parents, grand-parents, and us.

"We may be wrong, but all we ask is that you think about what we have said. If you have a different opinion and want to tell us how we're wrong, we'll listen. That's only fair. He's the only one of your friends who treats us like that."

Frankly, our explanation took a great deal of control on our part. It was important that we didn't act angry, hurt, or bitter. And we admit that we were tempted to express these emotions. We tried to keep in mind our goal, which was to indicate reasons for rejecting the one boy while contrasting his behavior with another of our grandson's friends.

We're quite sure that our grandson listened because *we kept the focus on our feelings.* Hopefully, he would be able to make a judgment based on what we said. No one wants to be ordered around! Since then, on any number of occasions, our grandson has said teasingly to us, "The friend you people like and I have plans. Are you happy?"

Whenever we discuss the need for tact, diplomacy, caution, and avoidance of attack in trying to discourage teenagers from continuing with friends or groups that can only hurt them in life, some parents question such an approach. "I disagree," said one woman. "I'm my son's mother, not some outsider. I see no point in playing cat and mouse with the truth. My son's life is involved. What concerns him concerns me."

We would not for a moment disagree with this mother's assertion. Why do we strongly emphasize tact and diplomacy rather than handing out directives the way we did while our children were small? The main reason for this stylistic shift is recognition and acceptance of the fact that a teenager is no longer a child. *Parents have to change how and what they do*. They have to rethink the nature of the relationship. Of course, one is still a parent. But, in addition to a parent, one is a friend.

The idea of a teenager being one's friend was a dramatic turning point in our relationship with our children. When we thought of our sons moving from just being our children to also being our good friends, our behavior changed, and we had a greater impact on their lives.

Good friends don't ground each other when there is a problem. Good friends don't bark our criticisms. Good friends are supportive when relationships go wrong. Good friends are caring but not intrusive.

We recall a teenager who had a lovely singing voice and was asked one year to appear in summer stock, playing the lead role of Snoopy in the musical *You're a Good Man, Charlie Brown.* The small-town reviews were glowing. However, it was also true that members of the teenager's peer group in summer stock were getting stoned on drugs and running every physical and emotional risk in the world. His parents decided to drop everything and go to the scene. Yes, the worst was true for a lot of the kids, and these parents felt that their son ran risks they cared not to have him take.

Bewildered and concerned, knowing all sorts of "no's" and threats would not work, the father decided that he would be a *good friend* and hang out at the scene. He rented a motel room and invited his son to stay with him rather than go back each evening to the barrackslike theater dorms. Also, he suggested that they might have dinner together, and then the son would be free to go wherever he liked. The father had brought along work and set up a temporary office in the motel room.

For four agonizing days the father chatted with his son and made himself available to talk. He was the "good friend" on the scene, a **ballast** in the midst of the entire chaotic, theatrical world. After four days, the son appeared early in the afternoon and suggested to his father that they return home.

"No problem," agreed the father. "I am ready. How about the performance tonight?"

"They can stuff it," said the young man.

With his arm around his son's shoulder, they walked to the car and returned home.

Support, caring, being the right sort of friend at critical times in adolescence can make all the difference as we personally know. The young man we just told you about was our son. Although we have made a strong pitch for diplomacy, tact, and making sure that no threats or coercion be used to make your child stop befriending undesirables, we think there is *one* time a different tactic must be used. If you have any hint that there is the possibility of drug or alcohol abuse, we strongly believe a passive role is one that just won't work.

Therefore, in the case of extreme dangers or substance abuse, we unhesitatingly urge parents to do whatever they can, seeking every resource to help their teenagers get back on track.

The tough question:

20 | *"What can I do to instill and reinforce ethical and moral values in my teenager?"*

"The day-to-day little things my teenagers sometimes do can be very irritating. They'll overspend or refuse to help with chores. No big deal. My husband and I can live with these problems. What I've come to realize is that the world won't fall apart if the grass isn't mowed. By and large they're great kids.

"What does concern my husband and me are **big** issues, questions of values, morality in a time when old-fashioned morality seems like a dead issue. I'm so confused about this. What do I do? My kids go to Catholic schools. We depend on teachers to teach them true Christian virtues. Is this enough? Can I do more?

"I wish I could be sure about what is getting across to them. I am honestly concerned about the decline of morality in the world. I know I can't wrap my kids in tissue paper and hide them from everything. Not that I want to, of course. But there's a lot out there I would prefer they didn't know about at their age. More than that, they need a firm base of morality if they're ever going to be productive, caring, and compassionate adults.

"A moral basis for life is a must. Even if the world around is a mess, having a decent set of ideals can be a source of strength. How do we get this message across to our children?"

Mr. And Mrs. O., parents of two teenagers,
seventeen and fourteen

The tough answer:

"What do you want most for your adolescents?" Fifteen years ago we asked parents this question. An overwhelming number listed **happiness** and **achievement** as their first choices. In preparing this book, we again surveyed parents. While it is true that happiness and achievement were frequently cited, a vast majority of parents also mentioned the importance of kids having a moral and ethical base to make their lives more meaningful. This change might possibly reflect society's changes in morality or what is publicized in the media.

"The righteous walk in dignity," one parent told us. "I want my son to be able to hold his head up high. You can be the smartest person, the best athlete, the best of everything, but, if your 'core' is bad, the rest means nothing."

We think all of us agree. How does one achieve this goal? Obviously, the first place to start is in the home. Parents, as we all know, are always providing instruction of some sort or another. As *one* example of morality and ethical instruction, we remember lecturing our kids about honesty, the need to be truthful, not to hide behind lies because, in the end, you'll only get caught.

We assumed that if we repeated ourselves often enough the message was bound to make an impression. Generally, this seemed to be the case. But what we also later discovered is that *our* cautions *carried far more weight than anything we ever said. Words alone can never be a substitute for concrete behavior.*

We learned this lesson from one of our sons. It so happened that he told a couple of "white" lies, the euphemism we all use to describe lying that we like to believe really isn't major. He was supposed to be at soccer practice. Instead, he was off buying more junk comics from a variety store. Knowing our feeling about such a waste of money, it was only natural that he covered all this up.

Instead of being truthful, he told us that he had stayed in school to help a teacher. Since helping teachers ranked high on our value list, he was sure that this was a good choice of an excuse. Hopefully, he would be spared one of those interminable, serious lectures his parents, with forefingers raised, typically gave in such situations.

It didn't work. We had the comic books as evidence. There was no escape. He had to stand and listen to a sermon about how little lies lead to big lies, and the truth comes out anyway. It was far better to be truthful right from the start.

"So even little white lies are wrong?" he asked.

"Of course."

"Even if the little white lies don't really hurt anyone?"

"Certainly."

"So the little white lie you told last week at the movies was wrong."

"The movies?" We struggled with our memories.

"Maybe we should forget about what I did," he said soothingly, "and I'll forget about what you did. We can *all* start over."

The four of us had gone to the movies, one sixteen-year-old son and this son, a *very* little over twelve years old. A sign on the window in large block letters clearly stated: children *under* twelve half price. "Three adults and one child," we said, pushing money under the cashier's window.

A long line of patrons waited behind us.

"You forgot," said our son, tugging a sleeve.

"Forgot what?"

"I'm already twelve. You told the lady three adults and one child."

No reply on our part. He was just *one* month past twelve. If only the sidewalk could have parted and swallowed us. If only the people behind us had been deaf. A lot of "if only's" crossed our minds as we added money to cover the additional cost.

Clearly, one way teenagers develop a sense of right and wrong and a set of ethical and moral values is by observing what their parents do and modeling their behavior on parents' actions. We learned that the values reflected by day-to-day parental behavior are likely to have a much greater effect on a teenager than abstracts about honesty or any other value.

But, of course, parents are by no means the only influence in a teenager's life. The social environment outside the home is also likely to play a part in the values your teenager acquires. This second insight became abundantly clear to us when one teenage son was a college freshman.

A little background information is needed to clarify this example. For whatever reason, as parents we had never been actively concerned with environmental issues. Of course, we aren't out to destroy the wilderness. We like trees, flowers, nature, clean air, a nice environment, but we never march, petition, or do anything on behalf of such matters. Whether people recycle or not, we note with some embarrassment, has not been one of our major interests.

Thus, we had no idea of what other people were doing with respect to teaching our kids. One weekend we drove over to visit this son. As we chatted, walking around the campus, every few minutes our son paused to pick up empty soda cans, cigarette butts, chewing gum wrappers, and other trash.

"They pay grounds people to clean up the litter," we said, a shade of irritation in our voices, thinking about how much tuition and room and board cost.

"But it's wrong," he told us. "*You people may not care* but we're all responsible for the environment everywhere." And he dove down behind a bush to retrieve another beer can. It turned out that, in one of his science courses, the professor had been spending some time lecturing and discussing about the need to preserve and respect the environment.

We conclude that if we want and expect our kids to be ethical and have moral values, then we have to behave consistently the way we want them to behave, not because of lectures but because of a desire to identify with us. On the other hand, we also have to expect that, with some matters, the outside world is going to be an important influence that may far outweigh anything we did or didn't do.

When a parent asked us, "Does religious education make a difference?" our reply was, "Certainly." Every association your teenager has in the right setting is going to be important. Belonging to the right group in the right church-related activities can go a long way in helping youngsters steer a moral course that will stand them in good stead the rest of their lives. What is important is for parents to do whatever they can to make sure that their kids are in the right environment, associating with people whose values they share.

A Final Word

Remember to keep the door always open. Despite what your kids do and say, despite the turbulence of the moment, let your kids know that you are always available to talk and, even more important, to listen.

Learn to live with and accept your parental humility. Forget about the ideal model of a perfect parent. It's far more important to be genuinely yourself, with your own faults and short-comings, but also with the honesty that can be achieved only by being true to yourself.

Encourage and reinforce your adolescent's striving for independence and individuality. Let your teenager grow up. This means respecting privacy, nagging a lot less, and working together as friends to achieve goals and to solve problems.

No matter what, *never never* give up on your teenager. Always be there in the good times and in those times when your teenager's world turns upside down and spins a little out of control.

Don't be afraid of making your values and feelings clear and explicit. Share your values and feelings and be willing to listen to your teenager's point of view. Remember that parents can learn, too. We don't have all the answers!

And last, but certainly not least, let your teenager know in whatever way you feel comfortable that you love him or her. Sometimes, we now realize, we forgot to say those magic words, *"I love you."*